WB 141

Analysing how we reach clinical decisions

Edited by

Huw Llewelyn

Senior Lecturer, Department of Medicine, King's College School of Medicine and Dentistry, King's College, London

and

Anthony Hopkins

Director, Research Unit, Royal College of Physicians

MEDICAL LIBRARY
WATFORD POSTGRADUATE
MEDICAL CENTRE
WATFORD GENERAL HOSPITAL
VICARAGE ROAD
WATFORD WD1 8H

D1464884

1993

ROYAL COLLEGE OF PHYSICIANS OF LONDON

Acknowledgements

This book is the outcome of a workshop sponsored by the Research Unit of the Royal College of Physicians, and held at the College. A list of participants is given in Appendix 2. Background papers were prepared and circulated in advance, and modified for this book in the light of the discussions at the workshop. We are grateful to the chapter authors and to all participants for their help.

The Research Unit of the College is supported by generous grants from the Wolfson and Welton Foundations, by other charitable donations to the College's Appeal Fund, and by the Department of Health.

Royal College of Physicians of London
11 St Andrew's Place, London NW1 4LE

Registered Charity No. 210508

Copyright © 1993 Royal College of Physicians of London
ISBN 1 873240 68 6

Typeset by Oxprint Ltd, Aristotle Lane, Oxford
Printed in Great Britain by Cathedral Print Services Ltd,
Rollestone Street, Salisbury SP1 1DX

Contributors

Lucio Capurso *Department of Gastroenterology, General Hospital, S. Filippo Neri, Via Martinotti 20, 00135 Rome, Italy*

Tim de Dombal *Director, Clinical Information Science Unit, University of Leeds, 22 Hyde Terrace, Leeds LS2 9LN*

Jack Dowie *Senior Lecturer, Faculty of Social Sciences, The Open University, Milton Keynes MK7 6AA*

Michael Drummond *Professor of Economics, Centre for Health Economics, University of York YO1 5DD*

Peter Emerson *Honorary Consultant Physician, Chelsea and Westminster Hospital, c/o 3 Halkin Street, London SW1X 7DJ; Director, Riverside Unit, Coding and Clinical Information System Development Project, London*

Graeme Hankey *Department of Clinical Neurosciences, Western General Hospital, Crewe Road, Edinburgh EH4 2YU, Scotland (Present address: Department of Neurology, Royal Perth Hospital, Box X2213 GPO, Perth, Western Australia 6001)*

Anthony Hopkins *Director, Research Unit, Royal College of Physicians, 11 St Andrews Place, London NW1 4LE*

Robin Knill-Jones *Senior Lecturer in Epidemiology, Department of Public Health, University of Glasgow, 12 Lilybank Gardens, Glasgow G12 8RZ, Scotland*

Maurizio Koch *Department of Gastroenterology, General Hospital, S. Filippo Neri, Via Martinotti 20, 00135 Rome, Italy*

Huw Llewelyn *Senior Lecturer, Department of Medicine, School of Medicine and Dentistry of King's College, Bessemer Road, London SE5 9RS*

Charles Pantin *Respiratory Physiology Department, City General Hospital, Stoke-on-Trent ST4 6QG*

James Slattery *Medical Statistician, Neurosciences Trials Unit, Department of Clinical Neurosciences, Western General Hospital, Crewe Road, Edinburgh EH4 2YU, Scotland*

Charles Warlow *Professor of Neurology, University Department of Clinical Neurosciences, Northern General Hospital, Ferry Road, Edinburgh EH5 2DQ, Scotland*

Editors' introduction

Huw Llewelyn and Anthony Hopkins

All doctors are familiar with the differences of opinion that exist about how to manage a particular condition, both about the general guidelines to adopt as well as what should be done for an individual patient. Guidelines may be arrived at by holding workshops or small conferences at which the scientific evidence for the effectiveness of interventions is reviewed. These often highlight deficiencies in available knowledge. There are often also differences of opinion, so there is a need to be able to focus clearly on why these differences exist. The same applies when an individual patient's care is discussed in a case conference or at a medical audit session. It is important therefore to be able to analyse the reasoning process which leads to diagnoses and decisions on clinical management. The discipline which addresses this issue is called 'clinical decision analysis', and draws on a number of other disciplines, especially probability theory and the assessment of the 'utility' or 'value' of outcomes of medical intervention.

Clinical decision analysis is not quite the same as computer diagnosis and other formal decision making methods such as expert systems, diagnostic algorithms and various ways of expressing guidelines in a logical way. These other formal decision making methods may also make use of probability calculations and diagrammatic representations, but they do so in order to arrive at a decision in a pre-arranged manner. Although clinical decision analysis uses the same techniques to make the decision making process explicit, it also breaks down the process into its component parts so that the effect of using different observations, actions, probabilities and utilities can be analysed. The analysis may be time consuming and could not be applied to every clinical decision. It can be useful in a complicated case where a simple guideline cannot be applied because of some uncertainty or disagreement. It is its systematic approach which makes clinical decision analysis an example of formal clinical decision making.

Clinical decision analysis depends on someone with clinical expertise examining the problem first, and then simplifying and structuring it so that it becomes amenable to a quantitative analysis. Formal decision making methods in general, and decision analysis in particular, can be thought of as an explicit framework which can be built around what has been conceived by the imagination, thus consolidating its conclusions. These formal approaches can thus be used to check decisions based on subjective impressions. If this were done habitually, it would have a powerful educational effect.

Medical audit in its present form takes place *after* any intervention. In future, it might be possible for a computerised audit to take place using a formal decision making process *before* a decision is implemented. Thus, if the clinical perspective and the guideline are in agreement, there will be a greater expectation that the anticipated outcome will be successful. If there is a discrepancy, this may be because the guideline or formal decision is wrong. Whatever the reason, there will be a smaller expectation of a successful outcome and the physician would proceed with special care. At the very least, a discrepancy should lead to a review of the clinical impression or plan.

Few decisions are final in medicine. They are usually followed up and, if the patient is not progressing as well as expected, another decision may be made to try a different approach. Clinical care in this sense is like a feedback process, reminiscent of the body's own reparative and homoeostatic processes. Indeed, the physician could be regarded as providing external supplementary feedback mechanisms which complement those of the patient. This feedback model of clinical care might be more appealing to a physician than a model based on statistics or logical algorithms. However, each 'feedback response' will depend on a decision, and these decisions depend on logic and statistics.

The decision about how to deal with a particular patient may be made from different points of view. It is entirely the patient's point of view which will be considered in this introductory book. In the UK, most patients do not have to take the cost of care into consideration, but this may have to be done in other parts of the world. A decision can also be considered from a hospital or departmental manager's point of view. For example, if a limited number of beds is available, a priority decision may have to be made as to who should be admitted. A doctor may have to make a decision which combines both points of view. Decision analysis allows decisions of this kind to be made explicit.[1-3]

The plan of the book

Chapter 1 considers the technological society in which we live, and the expectations of the general public and of government with respect to decision analysis and formal decision making methods. Chapter 2 considers the background and philosophy of clinical decision analysis and its relationship to other formal methods of interpreting clinical information. Chapter 3 presents a clinical case history, and shows how some of the principles outlined in Chapter 2 are applied to a real-life problem. Chapter 4 presents Bayes' theorem and its application to obtaining the probabilities used in clinical decision analysis. Chapter 5 analyses the characteristics of individual tests which make them useful during diagnostic and decision making.

Chapter 6 returns to a detailed discussion of the original case history together with a review of the relevant scientific literature, which shows how a clinician uses the available literature to formulate clinical decisions. Chapter 7 presents a detailed clinical decision analysis based on the construction of a comprehensive decision tree using the data reviewed in the previous chapter. Chapter 8 describes the practical steps involved in setting up a clinical decision aid which can be used in conjunction with a clinical decision analysis.

Chapter 9 introduces some broader issues, beginning with the importance of obtaining the patient's views on the value or utility of various outcomes, not only for clinical decision analysis but also for all other forms of clinical decisions. Chapter 10 reviews the different methods for arriving at utilities. Finally, Chapter 11 describes how clinical decision analysis might be used in conjunction with other formal methods of interpreting information in day-to-day clinical practice and research, and how these methods might be provided on the future 'clinical workstation'.

References

1. Eddy DM. Clinical decision making: from theory to practice. Cost effectiveness analysis. A conversation with my father. *Journal of the American Medical Association* 1992; **267**: 1669–75
2. Eddy DM. Clinical decision making: from theory to practice. Cost effectiveness analysis. Is it up to the task? *Journal of the American Medical Association* 1992; **267**: 3342–8
3. Eddy DM. Clinical decision making: from theory to practice. Cost effectiveness analysis. Will it be accepted? *Journal of the American Medical Association* 1992; **268**: 132–6

Contents

Page

Acknowledgements ii
Contributors iii

Editors' introduction v
The plan of the book vi
References vii

1 **Medical decision making, clinical judgement, and decision analysis**
  by Tim de Dombal 1
  Conclusion 4
  References 5

2 **Clinical decision analysis: background and introduction**
  by Jack Dowie 7
  Modes of judgement and decision making . . . 8
  The key questions in clinical decision making . . . 12
  System aids 13
  Clinical decision analysis: an introduction . . . 15
  Summary of the steps involved in a clinical decision analysis 19
  Another example of clinical decision analysis . . . 20
  Evaluating judgement and decision making technologies . 21
  Conclusion 24
  References 25

3 **A case history and some definitions**
  by Huw Llewelyn and Anthony Hopkins 27
  The case history 27
  Discussion 28
  The concept of 'probability' 30
  The concept of 'utility' or 'value' 31
  Estimating utilities 32
  Combining probabilities and utilities 33
  Decision trees 36
  References 38

4   The role of Bayes' theorem in diagnosis, prediction and decision making

by Robin Knill-Jones   39

Logical diagnosis   40

Statistical diagnosis   41

Algorithms and decision analysis   49

Conclusion   49

References   50

5   Analysing the discriminating power of individual symptoms, signs and test results

by Maurizio Koch, Lucio Capurso and Huw Llewelyn   .   .   51

The diagnostic process   51

The likelihood ratio   52

Weight of evidence   53

The pre-test probability.   54

The diagnostic 'gold standard'   54

The indices of discrimination   55

Distributions of test results   60

Reproducibility and accuracy of a test result   .   .   .   62

Meta-analysis   63

Reading a paper on the discriminating power of a test   .   65

Conclusion   66

References   67

6   A physician arriving at diagnoses, predictions and decisions

by Graeme Hankey, James Slattery and Charles Warlow .   .   69

Establishing the diagnosis   69

Anatomy of the transient ischaemic attack   .   .   .   72

The cause of the transient ischaemic attack   .   .   .   74

What is the risk of stroke and other vascular events? .   .   77

How to treat the patient   77

What are the risk factors?   77

Antiplatelet agents   88

Anticoagulation   89

Carotid endarterectomy   91

Addresses for entering patients into trials   .   .   .   93

References   94

7 **Clinical decision analysis: an application to the management of an elderly person with hypertension who has had a transient ischaemic attack**
by Jack Dowie, Graeme Hankey and Huw Llewelyn . . 99
Structuring the case 100
Assessment of probabilities and utilities 101
Calculating the optimal strategy 105
Conclusion 108
Reference 109

8 **Practical steps in setting up a decision support system**
by Peter Emerson and Charles Pantin 111
Definition of the domain of the decision aid . . . 111
Definition of first-phase indicants 112
The first prospective study 112
The prototype decision aid 113
Further trials 114
Field testing 114
Maintenance and quality control 115
Conclusion 115
Acknowledgement 115
References 116

9 **Practical guidelines and bringing the patient into clinical decisions**
by Anthony Hopkins 117
The patient's perspective 117
Discordances between the patient's and medical
  perspectives 118
Measurement of functional status 119
Practice guidelines 120
Conclusion 123
References 123

10 **Estimating utilities for making decisions in health care**
by Michael Drummond 125
Methods for obtaining valuations of health states . . 126
Measurement of utilities 126
Valuations of health states reported in the literature . . 131
Current methodological debates 133
Practical issues in using health state valuations . . 136

Conclusion   141
References   142

**11   Decision analysis in the context of day-to-day
      clinical practice, audit and research**
      by Huw Llewelyn   145
Analysing, explaining and checking decisions .   .   .   145
The decision   146
The diagnosis   147
The presenting complaint   147
Diagnostic evidence   149
Justifying decisions objectively   152
The expert's system   153
Conclusion   155
References   156

APPENDICES
1. Clinical decision analysis: an application to the
management of an elderly person with hypertension who
has had a transient ischaemic attack   .   .   .   .

                                                                                      157

2. Members of the workshop   163

1 | Medical decision making, clinical judgement, and decision analysis

Tim de Dombal*

Throughout history the practice of medicine has involved the making of judgements and decisions. The word *medix* is an ancient one, dating back to Etruscan times, and in those days had nothing to do with health care. A medix was a local magistrate, one who sat in judgement on local difficulties and problems, and made decisions in the best interests of the parties concerned.

Until recently, there has been little impetus within the profession to study or question the ways in which its decisions are made. Most medical decisions did not consume much in the way of resources and, probably until the last century, most of them did not significantly affect patient outcome. The accumulated wisdom of the medical profession was taught and learnt in a long, but relatively simple, system of apprenticeship, so that the decisions of relatively inexperienced doctors were effectively those of their peers. By the standards of the times, this system worked as well as could be expected, and there was little need or pressure to evaluate, let alone alter, the established procedure.

In recent years, this comfortable situation has been turned upside down, partly arising from societal pressures. In the light of the vastly increased potential for investigation and treatment of patients, society has in the last few decades come to realise the need to impose cost constraints upon the delivery of health care. Unfortunately, this has occurred at a time when the age of the population is increasing and, with it, the need for care. Public awareness and expectations have also both increased, stimulated no doubt in part by the daily diet of high technology and high cost medical care demonstrated in the media.

The traditional ways of teaching and making medical decisions have also been overturned by the complexity of modern medicine and the educational dilemmas that this creates. In the UK, the medical course is of finite length, and during the 1980s (according to information from the Committee of Vice Chancellors and Principals) the combined medical faculty has declined by 9.6%.[1] If the explosion of knowledge relevant to appropriate medical decisions for individual patients is set

*Clinical Information Science Unit, University of Leeds.

alongside these figures, it is not difficult to understand why hitherto effective traditional methods of making medical decisions and of teaching medical decision making have become inappropriate.

On a more positive note, there has been a surge of interest in the decision process adopted by doctors in the diagnosis and management of patients under their care. For many, however, this new interest in and study of medical decision making has been a source of discomfort. It is never comfortable when cherished and traditional beliefs and procedures are subjected to the fierce light of public debate and scrutiny, particularly when many of those conducting the scrutiny are not members of the medical profession and tend to speak in language and scientific jargon appropriate to their own disciplines but incomprehensible to doctors.

The explicit study of medical decision making and the introduction of more formal decision processes are both inevitable in the light of the preceding remarks and likely, it can be argued, to be beneficial to the patient, society and the public purse. Many physicians are wary of formal techniques such as decision analysis, which is both natural and understandable. Even quite junior physicians have spent a minimum of five or six years painfully and laboriously acquiring the knowledge they possess. Human nature being what it is, they are reluctant to adopt a technique which appears, at least at first glance, to entail them going back, so to speak, to square one.

Remembering the story of the famous ass which starved to death when placed equidistant between two piles of hay, they may well argue that adopting formal decision making techniques may actually impair the decision making process by causing the physician to agonise over each decision, thereby increasing the physician's stress and eventually leading to worse rather than better decision making. Of course this *should* not happen, but it is possible and there must be sympathy for the physician taking life-and-death decisions on a daily basis, often under conditions of great uncertainty.

Such worries about decision analysis are understandable and often unspoken; they emphasise the need for both the technique and the results of decision analysis to be presented to such a physician clearly, concisely and sympathetically, rather than, as on occasion in the past, competitively or confrontationally. Unfortunately, some of the worries which *are* expressed are often fallacious, and have led in the past to a gulf between the fraternity of decision analysts and practising physicians. It is worth discussing some of these worries at this point.

A view often expressed is that matters are reasonably satisfactory at the present time, and there is no evidence that formal decision techniques can improve performance. In fact, neither statement is true. The Panglossian presumption that we are already in the best of all possible worlds as far as decision making is concerned is simply not justified. To give one example, it is difficult to see how surgeons could have persisted with radical or supraradical mastectomy for decades if the management of breast cancer had been thoroughly and objectively explored using decision analysis techniques, in particular questioning the women concerned about the utility for them of the various outcomes.

Most diagnostic technologies, in distinct contrast to drug therapies, have not been subjected to objective evaluation. Many of them would never have been adopted on a wide scale had they been so subjected. Diagnostic accuracy amongst inexperienced doctors is falling. For acute abdominal pain it is 35–40% in the UK, and amongst the lowest in Europe.[2] The pick-up rate for gastrointestinal cancer at the first hospital visit is 44%.[3] The lead time from presentation to a physician with symptoms subsequently shown to be due to caecal cancer and firm diagnosis is around 48 weeks.[4] One-third of admissions to coronary care or intensive care wards with 'myocardial infarction' have no cardiogenic cause for their pain. By contrast, one in eight patients with a cardiogenic problem presenting to an emergency department have been seen somewhere else and sent away.[5] Of course, all this happens at 'other hospitals' but, by definition, that is where most physicians work.

Fortunately, there is now good evidence that, where sensibly introduced into routine clinical practice, the results of formal decision aids and detailed scrutiny of the clinical decision in a particular area are followed by improvements in performance, particularly amongst inexperienced staff.

In relation to acute abdominal pain, the careful report by Adams showed that when the findings of detailed studies were made available to inexperienced staff, performance improved in a number of hospitals (Table 1).[6] Similarly, application of a decision analysis to the diagnosis of acute chest pain and its management resulted in a false positive rate of 15% and a false negative rate of only 4%, in contrast to the figures outlined above.[7] Similar analysis reduced the lead time from presentation with gastrointestinal cancer until firm diagnosis from a median period of 24–52 weeks to 30 days.[8]

Thus, the argument that decision analysis and the study of clinical decision making is unrelated to reality or routine practice ignores a significant body of evidence. The evidence also disposes of a further argument, so often advanced by quite senior clinicians, that 'they do this anyway in their head by instinct'. This may (just, on occasion!) be true for senior clinicians, but the evidence confirms that it is *not* true of junior clinicians.

Other arguments advanced against decision analysis range from the confused to the bizarre. The argument that the physician mistrusts computers and numbers is often advanced, as is the argument that the

Table 1. Summary of findings in a recent Department of Health and Social Security trial of a computer-aided decision support-system for acute abdominal pain.

	Baseline (4,075 cases) (%)	Trial period (12,662 cases) (%)
Initial diagnostic accuracy	45.6	65.3
Post-investigation diagnostic accuracy	57.9	74.2
NSAP patients admitted from accident/emergency	40.9	26.3
NSAP patients who re-attended accident/emergency	7.4	1.5
NSAP patients operated on	9.5	5.6
Perforated appendicitis rate	23.7	11.6
Annual saving		
Negative laparotomies	—	139*
NSAP bednights	—	3,387*
Appendicitis bednights	—	871*
Bad management errors	0.9	0.2
Death	1.20	0.92

*Patients
NSAP = non-specific abdominal pain (not needing surgical treatment)
Reproduced, with kind permission from Ref. 3.

physician is reluctant to use results from an analysis the mechanism of which he or she understands only poorly. Yet the same physicians will happily base their case management upon a series of biochemical tests, or upon the results of computerised tomography scanning or magnetic resonance imaging—the detailed mechanism of which is certainly poorly understood by most physicians. As for the argument that physicians mistrust computers because 'life is too important to be left to a computer decision',[9] it has been observed elsewhere that when an aircraft turns on to its final approach, the wheels go down and neither the passengers nor the pilot can yet see the ground. If they truly believe that life is too important to be left to a computer, then this is a good time to get out and walk.

Conclusion

It has been demonstrated in the preceding paragraphs that the recent surge of interest in formal decision aids and the study of the ways in which physicians make decisions have come at an appropriate and relevant time. The demand for resources is increasing at the same time as constraints upon resource usage are becoming increasingly imposed upon physicians. Investigations are becoming more extensive, expensive and invasive, at the same time as the need for cost control increases. Meanwhile, the general public, ever more informed, is increasingly demanding that medical decisions should be explained to them.

The presumption that only 'fine tuning' of practice is needed is not justified. Throughout clinical medicine, there is increasing evidence of poor decision making which can be improved by the sensible application of formal decision techniques to the clinical area in question. In view of this, it is clearly of great importance that as many practising physicians as possible should have an understanding of these formal techniques, in particular decision analysis, and of how they can benefit themselves and their patients.

References

1. Committee of Vice-Chancellors and Principals, and Universities Funding Council. *University management statistics and performance indicators in the UK*. 1990 edition
2. Pera C, Garcia-Valdecasas JC, Grande L, de Dombal FT. European Community acute abdominal pain project meeting report, 10–12 March 1991, Barcelona. *Theoretical Surgery* 1991; **6**: 188–91
3. MacAdam DB. A study in general practice of the symptoms and delay patterns in the diagnosis of gastrointestinal cancer. *Journal of the Royal College of General Practitioners* 1979; **29**: 723–9
4. Clamp SE, Wenham JS. Interviewing by paramedics with computer analysis: gastrointestinal cancer. In: Rozen P, de Dombal FT, eds. *Frontiers of gastrointestinal research. Computer aids in gastroenterology*. Basel: S. Karger AG, 1984: 110–8
5. Emerson PA, Russell NJ, Wyatt J, Crichton N, Pantin CF, Morgan AD, Fleming PR: An audit of doctor's management of patients with chest pain in the accident and emergency department. *Q J Med* 1989 Mar; **70**(263): 213–20
6. Adams ID, Chan M, Clifford PC, *et al*. Computer-aided diagnosis of abdominal pain. A multi-centre study. *British Medical Journal* 1986; **293**: 800–4
7. de Dombal FT, Clamp SE, Softley A, Unwin BJ, Staniland JR. Prediction of individual patient prognosis—value of computer-aided systems. *Medical Decision Making* 1986; **6**: 18–22
8. de Dombal FT, Morgan AG, Giles GR, *et al*. Early detection of GI cancer by physician's assistant and micro-computer. *Medical Decision Making* 1981; **1**: 459
9. de Dombal FT. Computer aided decision support in clinical medicine. *International Journal of Biomedical Computing* 1989; **24**: 9–16

2 | Clinical decision analysis: background and introduction

Jack Dowie*

'Clinical decision analysis' is a term that is used both in broad and in narrow senses. In its broad sense, it refers to a cluster of formal techniques for the modelling, measurement and evaluation of clinical inputs, processes and outcomes. In a narrower sense, clinical decision analysis refers to the modelling of a clinical decision in the form of a 'decision tree', and the carrying out of the processes necessary to 'fruit' and 'prune' the tree so as to identify the optimal course of action (or 'branch'). The techniques for interpretation of tests and evaluation of outcomes, which can be used in isolation, also take their place as necessary components of the more comprehensive process of clinical decision analysis. In this chapter, the term is used in the narrow sense, as indicated above, as one tool for analysing how clinical decisions may be reached.

In Chapter 3 a common clinical situation will be encountered: the management of a patient with hypertension who has probably had a transient ischaemic attack. Before becoming immersed in this particular clinical situation, it is important to stand back a little and see where clinical decision analysis is coming from. This will be vital in determining where it is seen to be leading and in what spirit it will be regarded and judged. Clinicians will undoubtedly feel it is wise to look at the provenance of a second opinion, whoever or whatever method provides it.

It is worth emphasising that each of the component words in the term 'clinical decision analysis' carries its particular significance. *Clinical* signifies that in undertaking a clinical decision analysis we are, like the practitioner, concerned with the optimal management of an individual case, which can be of particular value when planning medical audit or research. Decision analysis as a technique can be used for programme evaluation or policy formulation at a community or public health level, for example when deciding on a policy for screening, but it is then no longer *clinical* decision analysis. Clinicians will be well aware that it is

*The Open University, Milton Keynes.

imperative to keep in mind the distinction between the 'bedside' and 'broadside' use of the technique.

Decision denotes the cognitive preliminary to the action (or inaction) which is to follow *now*. It therefore embraces any type of 'wait and see' choice, the selection of which is correctly seen as a decision rather than as postponement of a decision. (There is no such thing as a postponed decision, only a decision to wait for a specified or unspecified time before a subsequent and new decision is taken.) 'Decision' is to be contrasted with 'judgement'. It involves *choosing* between alternatives, whereas judgement involves the *assessment* of alternatives. 'Clinical *judgement* analysis' is the term applied to the statistical modelling of clinical judgements, for example of the probability or severity of a condition.[1] Thus, the chances of surgical complications or the quality of life they imply may be *judged*, but a *decision* is taken whether or not to operate.

Genuine decision making always involves situations where the possible outcomes of action (including doing nothing) are, first, uncertain and, secondly, of differing desirability. Clinical decision analysis provides the framework within which the *judgements of chances* and the *judgements of desirabilities/undesirabilities* necessary for optimal choice can be made independently (to avoid the dangers of cross-contamination) and logically integrated.

Finally, *analysis* signifies that an *explicit and quantitative modelling using carefully defined concepts* is being undertaken, in this case of the causes and consequences of ill health and of the consequences of possible interventions. In everyday language, analysis is often contrasted, either favourably or unfavourably depending on the person, with intuition. Among students of judgement and decision making, such a black and white dichotomisation, accompanied by an equally black or white evaluation, has fallen out of favour. One of the most prominent frameworks, Kenneth Hammond's *cognitive continuum theory*, certainly contrasts analysis with intuition but sees them as the poles of a continuum on which all types of cognition, including all medical judgement and decision making, may be located.[2] Furthermore, no pejorative connotations are necessarily associated with either term or either end of the continuum.

Modes of judgement and decision making

Cognitive continuum theory proposes a two-dimensional framework for studying judgement and decision making (Fig. 1).

The *cognitive* dimension (from which the theory gets its name) focuses on how we think about the task, running from highly intuitively to highly analytically. It is the main object of interest here, but

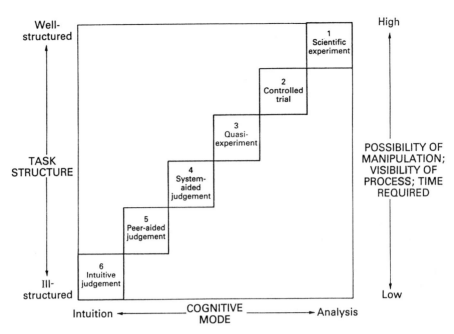

Fig. 1. *The cognitive continuum.*

Hammond's theory insists that attempts should not be made to address questions about this cognitive dimension (such as 'how analytical should be our thinking?') independently of the nature of the task being faced.[2]

The second, *task*, dimension accordingly focuses on how the task presents itself, running from very ill-structured to very well-structured. The characteristics which determine how ill or well a task is structured are numerous. It is sufficient for the present purposes to identify a few of them in a medical context. A domiciliary visit by a general practitioner to a previously unseen patient will confront him or her with a fairly ill-structured task in that many cues of a largely non-quantitative nature become available almost simultaneously. On the other hand, a consultant examining the latest test results for an inpatient who has been thoroughly investigated over several days is presented with a relatively much more structured task in that a few cues of a largely quantitative nature become available sequentially.

While the two dimensions are indeed continuous, Hammond's framework suggests that six broad modes of inquiry can usefully be identified when practices are located on both dimensions. At one extreme there is the classic scientific experiment of chemistry and physics which involves adopting a highly analytical approach to a very well-structured task. Progressively less well-structured tasks induce the progressively less analytical modes of the controlled trial and the quasi-experiment, the latter being particularly familiar to epidemiologists. All three modes provide much of the basic knowledge used by clinical practitioners, but they are not modes which clinicians practise as clinicians. The remaining three are the most clinically relevant ones.

Furthest removed from the scientific experiment is the mode labelled intuitive judgement and decision making, which involves using little analysis in approaching an ill-structured task. It is again emphasised that the term 'intuition' is used non-pejoratively, and that lack of analysis does not imply that extensive experience or knowledge is not being drawn on in some way. A more analytical approach to a somewhat better structured task takes us to the peer-aided judgement and decision making typical of the hospital setting. The need to articulate the case to colleagues is a prime reason for the higher analytical level characteristic of this mode.

The remaining mode, system-aided judgement and decision making (mode 4 in Fig. 1) is the prime focus here because it is the one in which clinical decision analysis in both broad and narrow terms is located.

System aid is here defined broadly to include almost any formal and explicit aid to reasoning directed at making judgements and decisions. System aids range all the way from highly sophisticated systems accessed by computer (including data-based scoring systems, knowledge-based algorithms and expert systems) to drawing on simple techniques such as, for example, listing logical possibilities on the back of an envelope.

One particular system aid which comes into use for the first time in mode 4 is the number system. It has been around for a considerable time and has been of considerable help in many tasks in which magnitudes of any sort are involved. Much medical discourse gives the impression that numbers are to be used when they are not. Some of the statements (of intention) that proliferate in mode 6, and particularly in that mode 5 form of decision making known as the 'meeting' or 'case conference', include the following:

- the home circumstances must be taken into *account*;
- the right *balance* must be struck between risks and benefits;
- there is a need to give considerations of quality of life proper *weight*;
- the claims of mother and baby must be kept in *proportion*.

The terms (charitably called 'verbal quantifiers') that are the common form in which assessments of chance or frequency are communicated among clinicians include the following: *rare, common, fairly likely, rather unlikely,* and a *reasonable chance.* There is however a relative lack of interpersonal agreement on the meaning of the terms.[3–5]

To complement these, other terms describe the severity of illness (severe, moderate, mild) and outcome (good, excellent).

At mode 4, the metaphorical and rhetorical use of the concepts of 'weighing', 'balancing', 'taking things into account' and 'establishing a sense of proportion' is replaced with actual, *numerical*, weighing, balancing and—literally—taking into *a count* and establishing *proportions*. Attempts to quantify verbally orders of magnitude, either of frequency or severity, are replaced by attempts to quantify them *numerically*.

Having explicitly (numerically) quantified what is otherwise implicitly and covertly quantified, the mode-4 practitioner is in a position to bring to bear (in the patient's interests) another set of valuable aids that have been the focus of sustained development for some centuries. These are the normative principles of mathematical and statistical reasoning—in a word, the principles of *calculation*. Clinical decision analysis should be seen simply as the logical framework within which human beings can specify the quantifications and calculations necessary for identifying the course of action that is in the patient's best interest.

Before looking more closely at how clinical decision analysis relates to the other forms of system aid that are becoming available in medicine, it is worth emphasising what will probably be obvious to any clinical reader. The six modes of cognitive continuum theory vary greatly in respect of how much control—ability to manipulate the variables in the situation—the judge or decision maker possesses. When human beings are involved, as they are in medicine, the possibility for controlled learning, even when motivated by concern for the patient, is much less than when studying a piece of rock. The modes also vary greatly in respect of the overtness and visibility of the inquiry process and hence in their replicability, the key characteristic of the scientific experiment, and accountability (defined here as the ability to give an account of what has gone on). Finally, and the most obvious to hard-pressed clinicians, they vary enormously in their requirements for time and resources, from virtually none at one extreme to almost unlimited at the other. The greater the time and resources available, the greater will be the analytical content of judgement and decision making according to the descriptive hypothesis of the theory.

The clinical reader is, however, also likely to have realised that these three determinants of the way in which a task presents itself to an individual practitioner are not outside human control, even if they may be outside that particular clinician's control. In any specific medical encounter they will be determined by such matters as governmental policies, the current state of the law, and relevant professional ethics and conventions. When a question such as 'what mode of practice is best for patients?' is asked, a consideration of the appropriateness of these contextual factors cannot be avoided.

The key questions in clinical decision making

It is helpful to distinguish the five different questions that may be asked regarding clinical judgement and decision making:

1. *How are clinical judgements and decisions made?* Answers to this question will take the form of descriptive theories such as that of Elstein *et al.*[6] and Eddy and Clanton[7] in medicine, and Hammond across the whole spectrum of making judgements and decisions.[2]

2. *How well are clinical judgements and decisions made?* Answering this question requires evaluative studies. These in turn require the development or adoption of some standard—and hence some valuations (ie value judgements). It is argued in question 4 that this is not a sensible question to ask, and that evaluations should take place only in comparative form.

3. *How could they be made?* This is another descriptive question, requiring an account of how alternative ways to the present ones of making judgements and decisions would work—for example, how various decision 'aids' or 'support systems' function.

4. *How well could they be made?* This is the proper comparative form of the evaluative question. It avoids the absurdity of non-comparative evaluation implied in question 2. The practical question in evaluation must always be whether a process performs better or worse than some well-specified alternative(s), even if the latter is only a random strategy such as tossing a coin.

5. *How should they be made?* This is a prescriptive or *normative* question. The answer may, in principle, bear no resemblance to what actually goes on, according to the descriptive investigations prompted by question 1. Clinical decision analysis is the application of a prescriptive theory. Its descriptive validity—whether practitioners do it or anything like it—is therefore irrelevant to its status, though not of course to its reception! Legal and ethical considerations will need to be brought in here, but only if they have not been—as they should have been—properly incorporated into the evaluations carried out in response to the previous question.

Interesting as some or all of these questions may be to psychologists, students of judgement and decision making, allocators of resources, managers, applied philosophers, *et al.*, clinicians will be disposed to take a practical interest in questions 3–5 — and indeed question 1 — only if the answer to question 2 is not 'pretty well', 'quite satisfactorily', 'as good as can be expected in the circumstances', 'not too badly, though a bit of fine tuning is needed', or something similar.

In Chapter 1, de Dombal has already indicated the indefensibility of such responses at a general level, even if there are doubtless pockets of exceptional practice. On both sides of the Atlantic, disturbing results have emerged both from studies of clinicopathological 'discrepancies'[8,9] and so-called 'small area variations'.[10] A burgeoning number of audit studies targeted on specific conditions, specialties or institutions has thrown up a substantial proportion of 'inappropriate' or 'unnecessary' procedures. 'We could do substantially better' is surely the appropriate generalisation, if one is to be made.

System aids

If the verdict 'could do substantially better' is accepted, what are the alternative modes of judgement and decision making that could possibly offer improvement? The broad answer, almost by definition, is system-aided judgement and decision making. Clinical decision analysis is our focus here, but there are other system aids available, and it will aid appreciation of what clinical decision analysis offers if it is set in the context of these alternatives.

Before doing so it is worth recalling that in talking about aids to judgement and decision making, we are talking about aids to information processing, not information provision. Aids which make more information available to the clinicians or make that information available in more accessible form are not aids to the (cognitive) information processing stage of concern here. This is not to say that they may not be a separate source of improved judgement and decision making.

The types of aid that have proved most acceptable to clinicians, even though this acceptance has been quite muted, have been knowledge-based. These take the form of either the algorithms/flow charts, now becoming familiar in the professional journals, or the expert systems which have absorbed considerable energy and resources in the past decade. Whatever their individual features, these aids draw on the sort of facts and assumptions about structures and relationships that clinicians themselves use, and can be seen as trying to make explicit (or at least mimic) best clinical practice. The internal reasoning is of the predominantly cause–effect or 'if–then' type that scientific medicine is often said to hold up as the ideal.

The other types of aid are those which are, broadly speaking, data-based rather than knowledge-based, whose claims to validity are based on statistical inference rather than on causal reasoning. Apart from some initial clinical input in the form of suggestions as to what are the possibly relevant indicants, such aids as the Leeds abdominal pain programme[11] and the Glasgow dyspepsia (GLADYS) programme,[12] rely on the purely statistical analysis of the relationships between indicants and disease(s) in a large number of patients in order to derive diagnostic probabilities. The outputs from such programmes can be made psychologically more appealing to clinicians by being presented in the form of weights of evidence for and against particular diagnoses (as in GLADYS), and they may contain some elementary medical knowledge in their branching logic, but this should not distract from their fundamentally statistical grounding.

Why should clinicians pay any attention to the results of what many see as 'merely statistical' analyses? Those on the other side of the 'clinical versus actuarial' controversy that has generated a vast litera-ture since the 1950s,[13] are in no doubt as to why they should do so—it would be in their patient's interest. This controversy relates to the comparative performance, over a series of individual cases, of unaided but expert human judges, on the one hand, and statistical models based on data drawn from similar cases, on the other. Meehl has written:

> There is no controversy in social science that shows such a large body of qualitatively diverse studies coming out so uniformly in the same direc-tion as this one. When you are pushing 90 investigations, predicting everything from the outcome of football games to the diagnosis of liver disease and when you can hardly come up with a half dozen studies showing even a weak tendency in favour of the clinician, it is time to draw a practical conclusion . . . If I try to forecast something about a college student, or a criminal, or a depressed patient by inefficient rather than efficient means, meanwhile charging this person or the taxpayer 10 times as much money as I would need to achieve greater predictive accuracy, that is not a sound ethical practice. That it feels better, warmer, and cuddlier to me as predictor is a shabby excuse indeed.[14]

The response of clinicians has often been that the studies are methodologically defective. Furthermore, many maintain that it is either impossible or unethical to undertake studies that would over-come these objections. Neither response is really effective.

The most interesting, but paradoxically the most neglected, form of aid in medicine, is the so-called bootstrap. This would be expected to appeal more to clinicians than the purely statistical aid, in that it is the result of modelling the relationship between the clinician's judgements and the disease, rather than modelling the relationship between indicants and disease (ie it involves, rather than completely ignores, the clinician). Here, too, the evidence from empirical studies is over-whelming: equations which capture the judgements of a clinician on a test set of patients outperform that judge when matched against him or her on a new set. The equation can capture what is valid in the judge's judgements and eliminate the invalid variability, or 'noise', arising from personal or interpersonal factors (such as offdays or difficult patients). Clinicians may be overconfident in their ability to integrate complex information more successfully than a simple formula. They may be reluctant to refrain from going 'beyond the information given' and to 'accept error in order to make less error'.[15]

Compared with any of these other types of aid, clinical decision analysis in the narrow sense used here has a unique advantage in providing for the explicit incorporation of individual patient values and preferences. It is the only method designed to aid decisions about individual patients as distinct from either aiding judgements about them (as do most data-based diagnostic aids) or, in aiding decisions about them, assumes that their values and preferences are identical (as do most knowledge-based algorithms or expert systems).

Clinical decision analysis: an introduction

Numerous examples of clinical decision analysis are to be found in the 'clinical decision making rounds at the New England Medical Center' section of *Medical Decision Making* from that journal's inception in 1981. They are also increasingly encountered in major specialty journals. A fairly random selection includes examples in cardiology (anticoagulant prophylaxis for thromboembolism[16]), paediatrics (management of infants at risk for occult bacteraemia[17,18]), physio-therapy (home versus clinic-based physiotherapy programme for patients with stiff shoulder syndrome[19]), and urology (radical prostatectomy versus radiation therapy in a patient with asymptomatic human immunodeficiency virus infection and stage B1 prostatic cancer,[20] or transurethral resection of the prostate versus 'watchful waiting' in cases of symptomatic prostatism[21,22]).

The key principle of all these, as of any decision analysis is, 'divide and rule'; that is, to break down the problem into its components, tackle these component tasks and then put the answers back together. They also embody the other central principles of 'measure' and 'maximise'. It needs to be emphasised that this is all to be done in pursuit of the professional goal of identifying what course of action is in the patient's best interest.

Any systematic exploration of a decision problem will necessarily involve the framing of the problem as a choice among alternative actions (eg to operate or not), with each action leading to a set of possible scenarios. Any one scenario will reflect particular resolutions of what is currently uncertain (eg the appendix was or was not diseased), and lead to a particular outcome state (eg good health or moderate disability). Decision analysis is simply the modelling of these key components of a decision formally in the form of a tree, of which the simplest clinically relevant example is presented in Fig. 2. The tree uses conventional notation. Choices are represented by square nodes, chance events (or uncertainties) by circular nodes, and outcomes by rectangles. This simple tree suggests that there are only two available options, here labelled 'remove', the other 'leave' (for example, a possibly diseased appendix or, to show the wide scope of the technique, a possibly abused child). It further suggests that there is uncertainty about whether or not the underlying condition is present and, finally, that there are four different outcome states, at least some of which will be regarded as more desirable than others.

This tree has also been provided with the numerical 'fruit' necessary for establishing the optimal decision: probabilities on the chance branches to quantify the uncertainties, and utilities on the outcome nodes to quantify the relative desirability or undesirability of the outcome states. The probabilities emanating from any chance node

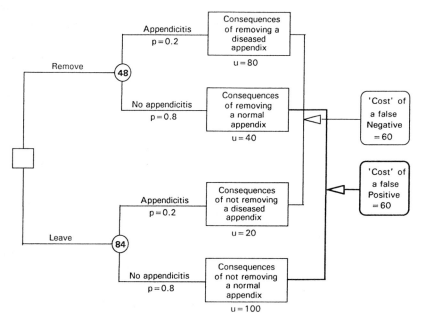

Fig. 2. *Decision tree.* The probabilities (p) and utilities (u) entered are purely illustrative. The expected utility (EU) of each option has been entered in its first chance node. This EU is calculated by weighting the utilities at each outcome node by their probabilities. For example, the EU of 'removing' is $(0.2 \times 80) + (0.8 \times 40) = 48$.

must add to 1.0 because they relate to mutually exclusive and collec-
tively exhaustive events. The utilities are simply values on a scale. This
scale has only interval properties, which means that while it is conventional to assign the least desirable of the possible outcome states to 0
and the most desirable to 100, this does not mean that the former is of
no value or the latter is perfect. The scale might equally have been
made to run between any two end-points, such as the 32–212° range of
the Fahrenheit temperature scale, but by common convention utility
scales usually run from 0–100 (or 1.0, as in Chapter 7).

Given the numbers inserted here, and acceptance of the principle of
maximising expected utility (weighting utilities by their probabilities),
the optimal choice is to 'leave'. Other numbers (and other principles)
could change this (eg a 50% probability of appendicitis will make
removal the optimal decision).

Adding a 'test' branch to such a decision tree (see Fig. 3) turns it into
a tree that can be an almost universal starting point for any clinical
problem. This is because a test includes any action designed solely to
yield information (ie anything from 'waiting and seeing' to magnetic
resonance imaging). The probabilities now identified as necessary for
calculating the optimal course of action include the predictive values of
positive and negative test results, which can be established by using
Bayes' theorem in conjunction with the performance characteristics
(likelihood ratios) of the test and the prevalence of the condition(s)
concerned. Fuller expositions of this probabilistic side of a decision
analysis are to be found in Chapters 4 and 5.

While this was not deliberate, the utilities entered in Fig. 3 show that
it is possible that testing will not emerge as the optimal course of action
even when a test is available. Indeed, as happens in both illustrations,
doing nothing may be the optimal course of action. There is no bias in
favour of doing something in clinical decision analysis, a point well
explored in the decision analytical study of oestrogen replacement
therapy by Elstein and others.[23]

Detailed expositions of clinical decision analysis, including the more
complex forms involving Markovian analyses of time sequences, are to
be found elsewhere.[24–28] It should be emphasised that there are few
limits to the complexity of decision trees. While many real-life cases are
more complex than the above illustrative and highly simplified ones,
the limitations of clinical decision analysis lie not in the technique, nor
in the computer software that is desirable for its implementation in
anything but the simplest case, but in the ability of human beings to
think clearly about and articulate great complexity. It is common to
find clinicians who argue that they cannot structure a problem in the
form of a tree (even with help from a specialist in decision analysis)

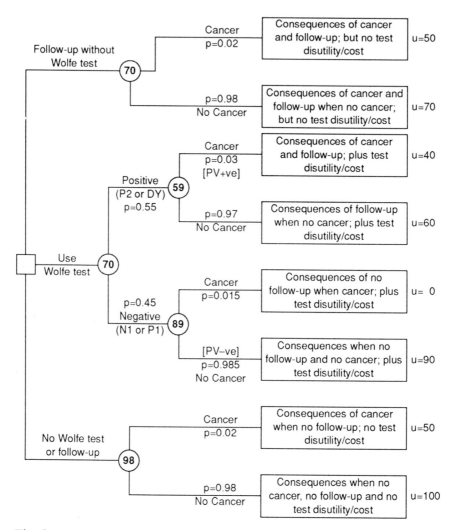

Fig. 3. *Decision tree with test branch.* The test concerned is the Wolfe typing of breast tissue. The probabilities and utilities entered are purely illustrative, though the former resemble the frequencies found in women referred to an actual breast cancer clinic in the UK (with 5–7 year follow-up). Wolfe codes: N1, normal fatty breasts; P1, a few prominent ducts; P2, lots of prominent ducts; DY, dense breasts. PV+ve, predictive value of a positive test result; PV−ve, predictive value of a negative test result.

because of the complexity of the problem, and arguing also that they cannot provide the logically necessary chance and desirability assessments. However, they still express confidence in their ability to make the decision successfully in a non-explicit, intuitive way. This is, of course, the sort of occasion on which the clash between modes 5 or 6 approaches and mode 4 approach becomes most overt.

Summary of the steps involved in a clinical decision analysis

1. Structure the problem as a decision tree, separating choices (what can be done) from information (what is and is not known) and preferences (what is and is not wanted). The tree is made up of choice and chance nodes and branches, and outcome states.

2. Assess (numerically) the probability of every chance branch, drawing on the literature, experienced colleagues and personal experience (in that order).

3. Assess (numerically) the utility of each outcome state, ideally eliciting the patient's own individual preferences (see Chapter 9). All the available techniques for doing this have their disadvantages, so again it is important to realise that we are not concerned with establishing 'the truth'—though that would be nice—but only with arriving at judgements which will produce a better decision than that achievable in any alternative mode.

4. Identify the option which maximises 'expected utility'; in other words, perform the calculations which weight each outcome utility by its probability and prune off all but the heaviest branch at each node. All this calculation and pruning can be done instantly by available software. The one choice branch that eventually remains is the optimal strategy, given the structuring and the various judgements made.

5. Carry out a sensitivity analysis to explore the effect of varying the judgements. This tests the robustness of the conclusion to changes in the data entered, establishing how small a change in any of the probability or utility assessments would result in a different option becoming optimal. This can help identify where further research efforts should be concentrated if time and resources are available. In many clinical situations the necessary time and resources may not be available. For example, if the analysis shows that a decision is affected by a small change in the prevalence of the target condition in the relevant population, it may not be possible to improve on the current best estimate within the relevant clinical time scale.

6. Literally 'toss-up' if two or more strategies tie for highest expected utility. Asking the patient to choose in this situation would suggest that there are relevant factors in his or her mind that have not been taken into a count in the analysis. If so, the analysis is defective. Of course, the patient may still feel happier to 'choose' in a toss-up situation, even though there would be no ground for regarding the result as a better decision.

Another example of clinical decision analysis

One further illustration will be given here to indicate the power of the technique to throw light on an important clinical decision. Barry and his colleagues compared the strategies of 'watchful waiting' (without intervention) and immediate transurethral resection (TURP) for continent, sexually active men with symptomatic prostatism (excluding those with chronic retention or large volumes of urine remaining after micturition).[22] Seventeen basic states were identified in which such men could be during each month with either strategy. The transition probabilities between these states were estimated from Medicare data and data gathered in the Maine Prostatectomy Study. The utility of each of these 17 states was estimated, with dead placed at 0 and 'asymptomatic after prostatectomy' at 1.0. The 15 intermediate utilities provide the necessary life-quality adjustments for the typical or 'baseline' case.

The baseline result of the analysis is expressed in terms of the expected number of quality-adjusted life months (QALMs) that each strategy would produce for a 70-year-old with moderate symptoms. The expectation from 'immediate TURP' was 122.91 QALMs ($10\frac{1}{4}$ years) and from 'watchful waiting', 119.97 QALMs (10 years), giving a net expected benefit from surgery of just under 3 QALMs. Most of this gain was accounted for by improvement in symptoms (+3.95 QALMs), with a little from prevention of urinary infection (+0.06), these increases being partly offset by the effect of operative risk (−1.07).

A sensitivity analysis revealed that this conclusion in favour of surgery was most sensitive to three variables: the operative mortality rate, the utility of the moderate symptomatic state, and the utility of impotence. This may appear obvious when stated, but it is much less apparent if not formally analysed and measured. Small changes in operative mortality rate or the value attached by patients to symptoms would alter considerably the results of the analysis.

The conclusions of Barry and his colleagues are worth quoting at some length, because they have serious, and by no means gloomy, implications for medical practice well beyond their particular context:

> The most important result [from this study] leading to a better understanding of variations in prostatectomy rates is the potent influences of the utility assignments [for 'moderate symptoms' and for 'impotence'] . . . An important implication of the dominance of these utility factors is that . . no truly definitive list of indications . . . can be promulgated and readily reviewed retrospectively to decide on the appropriateness of a surgical (or nonsurgical) recommendation. Patients must be asked about their preferences for outcomes, and these will differ for patients with similar medical histories, findings from physical examinations and

laboratory studies, and symptom levels . . . Further studies of patient utilities for functional outcomes following prostatectomy should help to preserve patient autonomy despite the great current pressures to stream-line and standardize medical practice . . . The informed patient who can make quality-of-life decisions based on his own preferences and attitudes towards risk may be our best safeguard against the concerns about cost and quality raised by variations in medical practice.[22]

Evaluating judgement and decision making technologies

I believe that the key question for the future of medical practice is the extent, if any, to which clinical judgements and decisions would be improved by increased adoption of system-aided techniques, in par-ticular by the adoption of clinical decision analysis as a normal part of the clinician's cognitive armamentarium. This question is evaluative and, to avoid the absurdity of non-comparative evaluation, requires comparative evaluation of alternative judgement and decision making 'technologies'. It makes little sense to try to evaluate broad alternative modes of clinical judgement and decision making in the abstract. The practical question is whether *this* particular implementation at mode 4 outperforms *that* at mode 5 or 6 (or indeed some other implementation at mode 4) (Fig. 1). An experienced clinician operating unaided in mode 6 *may* outperform even the best available mode 4 technology (eg himself using the most developed aid). Conversely, some junior or poor clinician *may* be outperformed by that most banal of all mode 4 approaches, the random device (coin, die). And of course a technology may be of a mixed-mode sort, as is the case with the Leeds abdominal pain programme. Its developer, de Dombal, has always suggested that it should be regarded as 'just another test' and that 'clinical judgement must always take precedence'.

Medicine is well attuned to the sort of comparative evaluation that is necessary. The controlled trial is as appropriate to the evaluation of decision technologies as it is to that of drugs or imaging technologies. While proper controlled trials are not always possible, it is essential that any compromises with the principles they involve should not be made in such a way as to favour a particular modality.

There is, however, an underlying question in this issue of evaluation that needs to be brought out into the open, not least because it is crucial to the proper comparative evaluation of clinical decision analysis: what does 'outperform' mean?

If the familiar structure–process–outcome framework is used, three main things can be evaluated and compared:

- inputs or structure, ie *what goes into* the alternative judgement and decision making technologies (eg the quality of the data used);

- process, ie *what goes on during* the alternative judgement and decision making technologies (eg whether the proper diagnostic inferences were drawn from the data provided); and

- outcome or result, ie *what was achieved* as far as the goal of the judgement and decision making was concerned, which in medicine would usually relate to the health state of the patient.

Which focus should be adopted or, if the answer is all three, what weight should be given to each when the answers from the three are conflicting? Surely we should judge by results? The racecourse perhaps offers an appropriate analogy. Before computers, the totalisator had separate windows for the placing of bets before the race and the collection of winnings after the race. Before the race, many people had high-quality information (eg from *The Sporting Life*), and many others possessed more or less sophisticated systems for processing that information into ratings of the likelihood of each horse winning. Others had no visible method for determining upon what horse they would bet, though a few clearly exhibited the equivalent of clinical judgement based on years of experience. The author's personal philosophy was to try to identify the people who were regularly to be found at the payout windows after the race and attempt to replicate their bets, irrespective of the inputs or process they used in deciding on them. This, he now realises, was evaluation by results, embodying no commitment to any inputs or process that could not be shown to have a desirable impact on the fundamental goal of the activity concerned. In advocating the adoption of technologies such as clinical decision analysis, it is in the belief that proper comparative evaluation by results *will* confirm their superiority. Comparative evaluation by results is just beginning, so in the meantime (and only in the meantime) the case must rest on comparative evaluation of process and input.

Is the distinction between inputs, process and outcome as clear in medicine as it is on the racecourse? For many, the answer will be a very loud 'No'. They will point to the high value that patients place on the *processes* which they experience as they pass through the health care system as distinct from the effect of treatment on their health state. There is a widespread confusion in this area, which is better resolved by recognising the importance of non-health outcomes rather than by introducing the idea that processes are valuable 'in themselves'.

Turning briefly to a very different culture from ours, the following appears on a placard in an exhibition about the Sepik river people in the Museum of New South Wales, Sydney, Australia:

> The Abelam people present an alternative to the [conventional] view of art. For them, painting is a magic procedure, where men are in com-

munication with the powerful and creative forces of the spirit world. Thus, the process of creating is as important as the final creation. It is therefore logical that, soon after the paintings and carvings are created, they are dismantled. They have served their purpose in providing a forum where men come in contact with the spirit world. They are too powerful, too secret, to be left in the village during everyday activity. They are destroyed without misgiving, for the Abelam know that others can be created.

On the surface, this would appear to be an excellent exposition and defence of the 'process utility' position: that satisfaction is obtained from processes as well as from outcomes. On the contrary, I think it enables the fallacy to be countered that outcomes are confined to the tangible, measurable and the observable. The outcome of a process is what we (humans) say it is. In the case of the Abelam people, the outcome is clearly not the utility of the physical object (as it is to art collectors) but the utility of the state of 'being in contact with their spirit world'. If a particular act or period of painting does not take them into that state, it will have failed as a process. By analogy, patients who wish to be informed and feel an autonomous part of the decision, will or will not be in the states of 'feel informed', 'feel autonomous', or feel them to some degree, depending on the adequacy of the process. Even processes such as 'information provision' and 'making the patient feel comfortable' can be evaluated only by their outcomes.

It is possible to argue that adopting formal decision processes such as clinical decision analysis will ensure better inputs into decisions. They will identify the data that are logically necessary for the decision but are not being collected or are currently of poor quality. (Much of the improvement in outcome produced by the Leeds programme on the management of abdominal pain is attributed to the discipline it enforced in history taking![11]) It can also be argued that, almost by definition, such formal techniques embody better or more correct processing of any inputs because, for example, they prevent clinicians confusing the probability of a disease given a symptom with the probability of a symptom given a disease. But the fundamental justification for regarding one process as better than another must surely be that it produces better results.

There are still deeper questions lurking: first, whose values or preferences are to be 'taken into account' (or 'taken into a count')? Secondly, within what contextual factors and constraints is the evaluation to take place regarding time, resources, legal standards, ethical principles, etc? In relation to these deeper level issues, the case for moving increasingly to mode 4 of Fig. 1 is simple. It is not that the solution or resolution of these questions will be easier. It is the fundamental case for explicitness and openness ('transparency') in the process of evaluation.

Conclusion

Concerns about or objections to clinical decision analysis are usually advanced as either practical worries or issues of principle, with the word 'ethical' usually making an appearance somewhere in the latter. At a practical level, can the complexity of real clinical cases be adequately articulated, even if there is agreement that we would like to do this? Can the 'probabilities' and 'utilities' for the decision tree be obtained? (The quotation marks signify that there are no such things as *the* probabilities or utilities in clinical medicine—just ones on which there is more or less intersubjective agreement.) Above all, will the time and resources be available to apply it? Ethically speaking, does clinical decision analysis infringe people's rights and/or ignore their obligations because of its fundamentally utilitarian–consequentialist nature? Apart from the question of whether the time and resources are available for clinical decision analysis, even if clinicians possessed the skills to carry them out, I intend only to acknowledge the legitimacy of these questions and conclude by making a final attempt to ensure that they do not divert attention from the central issue.

Time and resource constraints are real, and clinical decision analysis *can* involve extensive amounts of both. The bedside use of clinical decision analysis in acute medicine will inevitably be largely conceptual, its full quantitative rigour being reserved for cases that are of sufficient general interest to warrant the necessary research time and resources, ie where the 'baseline' analysis can serve as a provisional clinical policy for a broad range of patients. But clinicians will need to be familiar with the basic features of the approach whichever way it is used, either so that they can themselves attempt the limited analysis that is possible in the time available (to generate, in effect, their own second opinion) or so that they can understand full-scale analyses of relevant cases that have appeared in the literature or are offered to them as genuine second opinions.

Accusations levelled at clinical decision analysis—of subjectivism (in probability assessment), quantification of the unquantifiable (in utility assessment) and improper treatment of rights (in aggregation across parties)—undoubtedly have force, but the practical questions can only be:

- How does the *status quo* alternative deal with the problems to which such quantifications and calculations represent the clinical decision analysis response?

● Does the *status quo* alternative deal with them any better?

I have tried to address the ethics of clinical decision analysis elsewhere,[27] and will simply ask here whether it is ethical to assume that an individual's own unevaluated decision process is *necessarily* better than an alternative? The Greek forerunners of today's clinicians were constantly warning of the dangers of *hubris*, the tendency to exaggerate one's powers to the point where self was confused with the gods. At a more down-to-earth level, it would be wise to remember Hilly Einhorn's waiter who worked in a busy restaurant and had to decide to whom to give good service and to whom cursory service.[15] He made a judgement as to who would be good tippers and who would not, and served people accordingly. He found his judgement to be excellent!

References

1. Kirwan JR, Chaput de Saintonge DM, Joyce CRB, *et al.* Clinical judgement analysis—practical application in rheumatoid arthritis. *British Journal of Rheumatology* 1983; **22** (suppl): 18–23
2. Hamm RM. Clinical intuition and clinical analysis: expertise and the cognitive continuum. In: Dowie J, Elstein A, eds. *Professional judgment: a reader in clinical decision making*. Cambridge: Cambridge University Press, 1988: 78–105
3. Beyth-Marom R. How probable is probable? A numerical translation of verbal probability expressions. *Journal of Forecasting* 1982; **1**: 257–69
4. Kong AM, Barnett GO, Mosteller F, Youtz C. How medical professionals evaluate expressions of probability. *New England Journal of Medicine* 1986; **315**: 740–4
5. Nakao MA, Axelrod S. Numbers are better than words: verbal specifications of frequency have no place in medicine. *American Journal of Medicine* 1983; **74**: 1061–5
6. Elstein AS, Bordage G. Psychology of clinical reasoning. In: Stone G, Cohen F, Adler N, eds. *Health psychology—a handbook*. San Francisco: Jossey-Bass, 1979 (reprinted in Dowie and Elstein, ref. 28)
7. Eddy DM, Clanton CH. The art of diagnosis: solving the clinicopathological puzzle. *New England Journal of Medicine* 1982; **306**: 1263–8 (reprinted in Dowie and Elstein, ref. 28)
8. McGoogan E. The autopsy and clinical diagnosis. *Journal of the Royal College of Physicians of London* 1984; **18**: 240–3
9. Goldman L, Sayson R, Robbins S, *et al.* The value of the autopsy in three medical eras. *New England Journal of Medicine* 1983; **308**: 1000–5
10. Wennberg JE, Freeman JL, Culp WJ. Are hospital services rationed in New Haven or over-utilised in Boston? *Lancet* 1987; **i**: 1185–9
11. de Dombal FT. Computer-aided diagnosis of acute abdominal pain: the British experience. *Revue d'Epidémiologie et de Santé Publique* 1984; **32**: 50–6 (reprinted in Dowie and Elstein, ref. 28)
12. Spiegelhalter DJ, Knill-Jones RP. Statistical and knowledge-based approaches to clinical decision-support systems, with an application in

gastroenterology (with discussion). *Journal of the Royal Statistical Society, Series A* 1984; **147**: 35–77

13. Dawes RM, Faust D, Meehl PE. Clinical versus actuarial judgment. *Science* 1989; **243**: 1668–74

14. Meehl PE. Causes and effects of my disturbing little book. *Journal of Personality Assessment* 1986; **50**: 370–5

15. Einhorn H. Overconfidence in judgment. *New Directions for Methodology of Social and Behavioral Science* 1980; **4**: 1–16

16. Pauker SG, Eckman MH, Levine HJ. A decision analytic view of anticoagulant prophylaxis for thromboembolism in heart disease. *Chest* 1989; **5** (suppl): 161S–9S

17. Downs SM, McNutt RA, Margolis PA. Management of infants at risk for occult bacteremia: a decision analysis. *Journal of Pediatrics* 1991; **118**: 11–20

18. Lieu TA, Schwartz S, Jaffe DM, Fleischer GR. Strategies for diagnosis and treatment of children at risk for occult bacteremia: clinical effectiveness and cost-effectiveness. *Journal of Pediatrics* 1991; **118**: 21–9

19. Watts NT. Clinical decision analysis. *Physical Therapy* 1989; **69**: 569–76

20. Roach PJ, Fleming C, Hagen MD, Pauker SG. Prostatic cancer in a patient with asymptomatic HIV infection: are some lives more equal than others? *Medical Decision Making* 1988; **8**: 132–44

21. Krumins PE, Fihn SD, Kent DL. Symptom severity and patient's values in the decision to perform a transurethral resection of the prostate. *Medical Decision Making* 1988; **8**: 1–8

22. Barry MJ, Mulley AG, Fowler FJ, Wennberg JW. Watchful waiting vs immediate transurethral resection for symptomatic prostatism; the importance of patients' preferences. *Journal of the American Medical Association* 1988; **259**: 3010–7

23. Elstein A, Holzman GB, Ravitch MM, *et al.* Comparison of physician's decisions regarding oestrogen replacement therapy for menopausal women and decisions derived from a decision analytic model. *American Journal of Medicine* 1986; **80**: 246–58 (reprinted in Dowie and Elstein, ref. 28)

24. Weinstein MC, Fineberg HV. *Clinical decision analysis.* Philadelphia: WB Saunders, 1980

25. Doubilet P, McNeil BJ. Clinical decision making. *Medical Care* 1985; **23**: 648–62 (reprinted in Dowie and Elstein, ref. 28)

26. Dowie J. *Professional judgment and decision making: introductory texts 1–11. Course D300.* Milton Keynes: The Open University, 1991/92

27. Dowie J. Decision analysis: the ethical approach to medical decision making. In: Gillon R, ed. *Principles of health care ethics.* Chichester: Wiley, 1993

28. Dowie J, Elstein A, eds. *Professional judgment: a reader in clinical decision making.* Cambridge: Cambridge University Press, 1988

3 | A case history and some definitions

Huw Llewelyn* and Anthony Hopkins[†]

This chapter begins by describing a clinical case presentation, followed by a brief discussion exploring the probable diagnoses and decisions which will have to be made in order to investigate the patient and to begin treating her. The important terms and concepts introduced in Chapter 2 by Dowie are presented again in relation to a particular clinical problem in order to illustrate in more detail the principles involved.

The case history

A woman aged 70 who lives alone presents four hours after the sudden onset of weakness and clumsiness of the left arm which she noticed when brushing her hair that morning. By the time the physician sees her, some recovery has already taken place. There is no previous history of migraine, seizure or any other significant illness, and she has smoked five cigarettes a day for more than 40 years. When first examined, the left hand is clumsy, there is a mild weakness of the lower part of the left side of the face, and no signs elsewhere in the nervous system. On examination of the cardiovascular system, the pulse rate is 84 beats per minute and the rhythm is irregularly irregular. The blood pressure is 200/120 mmHg. There are no cardiac murmurs, but there is a bruit over the bifurcation of the left carotid artery (grade 3/6). The retinal arteries show mild arteriovenous nipping. Investigations reveal a normal chest X-ray with a slightly enlarged heart, and an ECG shows atrial fibrillation and moderate left ventricular hypertrophy. The blood sugar is 5.0 mmol/l, the serum cholesterol 6.7 mmol/l, the erythrocyte sedimentation rate 20 mm in the first hour, and the thyroid-stimulating hormone, 2.5 mu/l. Echocardiography shows no valvular disease or atrial thrombus. The Venereal Disease Research Laboratory (VDRL) test for syphilis is negative. On examination the following morning, the facial weakness and

*School of Medicine and Dentistry, Kings College London, and [†]Director, Research Unit, Royal College of Physicians.

hand clumsiness have entirely resolved, and a cranial computerised tomogram is entirely normal. Three days later the blood pressure is 170/105 mmHg, and it is the same two weeks later in the outpatient clinic without any treatment.

Discussion

A physician listening to this case history will regard the main problem as a sudden neurological deficit which begins to resolve rapidly over the ensuing few hours, and which resolves completely within 24 hours of onset. He or she will recognise this pattern of events as those of a transient (cerebral) ischaemic attack (TIA). The physician will also need to consider an unusual presentation of migraine, a fit or hypoglycaemia. However, the absence of any other features which also occur in these conditions (but not with a TIA) makes these other diagnoses even less probable. Indeed, the absence of these other features means that the recognised criteria for a TIA have been met. The fact that widely accepted criteria have been met means that all physicians who recognise and accept them will make the same diagnosis.

'Making a diagnosis' implies that a label has been attached to the patient or that the patient has been allocated to that group, class or set of patients called 'those with a TIA'. Such patients could also be allocated a diagnostic code. However, a diagnosis is not just a label, but also a term which summarises our imagination and understanding of what has happened to the patient. The physician's understanding will depend on other concepts which are familiar to him, drawn from his medical education and research, and his experience of observing similar patients in the past and what happened to them. All these past experiences will be used to imagine what is happening to the current patient's anatomy, physiology, biochemistry and, in particular, to the state of her vascular system and platelet function. These experiences will also be used to imagine what has happened to her in the past, and what will probably happen to her in the future with or without different types of intervention. The physician's imagination fills in the gaps between what he can see, feel and measure. The clarity and certainty of his imagination will depend upon the number of possibilities with which the clinical information is compatible.

In this patient's case, the physician may well imagine that she has suffered ischaemic damage to part of her right cerebral hemisphere, most of which will reverse and leave no detectable residual functional disability. The physician will imagine, first, that this could have been caused by a relatively small embolus lodging in a branch of the right middle cerebral artery, and then perhaps breaking up and being disseminated in blood vessels downstream and, secondly, that the embolus may have arisen from an area of damage of the vascular endothelium associated with turbulence of blood flow. The source of this embolus may have been an atheromatous plaque or the fibrillating left atrium. The patient's clinical findings are compatible with both possibilities, so the physician will dwell briefly on each in turn, remembering that the conventional treatment for preventing an embolus arising from a fibrillating left atrium is treatment with warfarin,[1] whereas prevention of a platelet thrombus arising from an atheromatous plaque is aspirin.[2] The physician needs to decide whether to recommend aspirin or warfarin, both or neither, and whether further investigations are required before so deciding.

The bruit is on the left side of the neck, which indicates that the patient may indeed have atheromatous plaques in this carotid artery, but perhaps in others too. However, the cause of this bruit cannot have been the source of the relevant embolus, because the embolus had lodged in the right hemisphere causing temporary symptoms and signs in the left hand. If there is a carotid lesion on the right side, it may not be sufficiently irregular or tight to cause a bruit. Alternatively, there may be a very tight stenosis on the right side, so that flow is limited and no bruit can be heard. A decision will have to be made whether carotid surgery will be feasible or desirable in this case, and whether further investigations such as Doppler ultrasound should be performed to pursue this possibility.

Other aspects of the patient's case history also need to be considered. The irregularly irregular pulse clinically suggests atrial fibrillation (which was confirmed by the absence of P waves and the irregularly irregular QRS complexes on the ECG). The pulse rate of 84 beats per minute means that digoxin is not required to control the fibrillating rate. Warfarin may be needed because of the risk of future embolus,[1] irrespective of whether this was the source of the embolus which caused the TIA on this occasion.

The blood pressure fell after admission, but remained moderately elevated after two weeks. The presence of arteriovenous nipping on fundoscopy, the enlarged heart on the chest X-ray and the evidence of left ventricular hypertrophy on the ECG all suggest that the hypertension had been present for many months at least.

The cholesterol level is mildly elevated (6.7 mmol/l), and the risk of a further vascular event is also increased by smoking five cigarettes a day. The physician will advise the patient about these risk factors but she may be reluctant to change her lifelong eating and smoking habits. If she did go to such trouble, she would expect to get some clear benefit. The decisions to be made with the patient will depend on estimating both the risk or probability of further vascular events of various severity and also the effect that different treatments and advice will have on these risks. These treatments will carry their own risks which need to be balanced with what the patient stands to gain.

In some instances it may be possible to modify the treatment at follow up. This is easier with drug treatment than with surgery, of course. For example, if the patient were to show early signs of gastro-intestinal bleeding, a previous decision to use, say, warfarin might be reversed. In this sense, the physician behaves as a 'supplementary feedback mechanism' to help the patient maintain homoeostasis and, as far as possible, the structural integrity of her body and her sense of well-being. Each attempt by the physician to compensate for a failing mechanism will need a decision of some kind. This concept of balancing risks with benefits in an explicit and logical manner when making such decisions, and the patient's involvement in doing so, is the subject of this book.

There are two closely related concepts about which to be clear: 'probability' and 'utility' (or 'value'). It is also important to understand the relationship between these two and how they are used to arrive at a combined measure known as the 'expected value' or 'expected utility'. It is the latter which determines the decision made jointly by the patient and her physician.

The concept of 'probability'

The ideal position for discussing any patient's case history would be in the light of extensive experience with a large group of similar patients, so that at any point in the history, examination and process of investigation there will always be a large number of previous patients with identical findings to the patient in question. This experience could then be used to make predictions with precise degrees of certainty. For example, if 80% of a large group of 70-year-old women with sudden weakness and clumsiness of the left arm and face on the day of admission which resolved within 24 hours, who also had a bruit on the left side of the neck, were found to have some degree of carotid artery stenosis on duplex ultrasound examination, it could be inferred that a new patient with the same findings has a 'probability' of 0.80 of also having a carotid artery stenosis on ultrasound. The value of 0.80 represents a degree of certainty in a prediction on a scale from 0–1.

Whenever a probability of 0.80 is attached to a number of predictions, 80% of them would be expected to be correct. A correspondence between estimated probability and subsequent experience is the hall-mark of good judgement. If, instead, only 30% of the predictions with probabilities of 0.80 (based on the large group of similar patients) were correct, the probability of 0.80 would have been over-confident. This difference represents poor judgement, in the sense that the physician was either inaccurately classifying patients or was misinformed about the true probabilities of outcome in a universe of similar patients. Alternatively, of course, a series of unpredicted outcomes may reflect poor care.

Well documented experience of previous patients is a precious and comparatively rare commodity. Because of this, it is difficult to talk reliably about degrees of certainty even in qualitative terms, let alone in terms of precise probabilities. As a result, it becomes necessary in clinical decision analysis to estimate or guess many probabilities. The methods for doing this are described in Chapters 4 and 5. Indeed, it sometimes is not possible to arrive at probabilities by basing them on past groups of identical patients because the combination of features displayed by a patient may be rare or even unique. In this situation, it may be necessary to calculate an estimated probability by making a number of assumptions which are difficult or impossible to test. However, although many assumptions cannot be tested, the final calculated probabilities can be tested by carefully recording subsequent predictions and checking (or 'auditing') whether the frequency of correct predictions matches the estimated probabilities. Although the need to estimate probabilities may compromise the accuracy of a decision analysis, it is still helpful to use estimated values as this serves to make the tentative reasoning process more explicit; it also helps to focus on those areas where the data are sparse. Chapter 6 reviews the literature for patients presenting with TIAs and discusses in detail the strengths and weaknesses of the data available. The process of estimating probabilities and using them in calculations is an important aspect of decision analysis and will be explained below and in Chapters 4, 5, 7 and 11.

The concept of 'utility' or 'value'

The outcomes for which the probabilities have so far been estimated refer to those which can be seen or measured by a physician or surgeon alone; for example, the discovery of the features of carotid stenosis at surgery or the fall of blood pressure to within some specified range after drug treatment. However, the most important groups of outcomes from the patient's point of view are future general health status and well-being, and the patient's valuation of that state. Outcomes of the latter kind, when taken together, correspond to the concept of 'utility' or 'value'. Clearly, these valuations can be experienced and reported only by the patient. General health state and sense of well-being are particularly difficult for the patient to report reliably because her sense of these over some length of time, for example, five years, would have to be considered. Her sense of well-being may also change from time to time due to factors unrelated to the condition for which she sought advice and for which she was being treated.

Another difficulty is that variation in mood and other aspects of pyschological life is greater than physical variation. For example, from clinical and imaging experience with previous patients, it might be possible to predict with a high probability the degree of residual paresis that a patient may experience after a stroke. However, in patients with the same degree of paralysis, the functional status and well-being can vary considerably depending upon their drive and ability to adapt, the domestic support they are given, the attitude of their peers and so on. The importance of these issues in day-to-day clinical practice is discussed in detail in Chapter 9.

The classical approach taken in clinical decision analysis is to ask the patients to estimate the future utility or value for themselves of various outcomes of clinical management. This is based on the assumption that patients' personal experience of how they have dealt with other events in their life will provide a more accurate estimation of utility to them than the experience of doctors with other patients with the same disease and similar attributes. Nevertheless, the exercise can be carried out on behalf of a patient by a relative or doctor—which is necessary if the patient cannot communicate because of unconsciousness. This process of estimating future well-being is known as 'estimating utilities'. It is described in detail in Chapter 10, but will be introduced here because a basic understanding of the concept is assumed in earlier chapters.

Estimating utilities

The physician describes to the patient the nature of the outcome in detail. This may be supplemented by written material, by arranging for the patient to meet others who have experienced the procedure and outcome, or perhaps by the use of video-recordings.

Let us consider the case of hemiplegia after stroke. The patient can be asked to imagine that she has a choice of entering two doors.[3] If she goes through the first door (the 'certainty of stroke' door), she will have to live the life of someone who has suffered a stroke. However, if she goes through the second (the 'kill or cure gamble' door), there is a 50% chance that she will die (a state regarded as having a utility of 0) and a 50% chance that she will be perfectly well and lead a normal life (a state regarded as having a utility of 1).

The patient is now asked to choose between the two doors. If she is indeed able to choose, say, the 'kill or cure gamble' door, the question is rephrased by changing the chances of dying or leading a normal life say, to a 60% chance of dying and a $(100 - 60) = 40\%$ chance of leading a normal life. If she is unable to choose between either door, this response is taken to mean that she regards a probability of 0.4 of a cure, and thus leading a normal life, as being equivalent in her mind to a utility or value of 0.4 (on a scale of 0–1) for living the life of someone who has suffered a stroke. This is how the original concept of utility was proposed by von Neumann in terms of indifference about wagers.[4]

A utility may also be viewed as any measurement of outcome and on any scale. This could be a subjective measure of well-being marked by the patient on an arbitrary continuous scale (eg from 7–77). The resulting measurement could then be treated mathematically like any other measurement, such as body weight or blood cholesterol level. For example, if 60% of patients had a severe stroke with a well-being score of 37, and 40% of patients had a mild stroke with a well-being score of 57, the average well-being score for the whole group would be

$$\frac{(60 \times 37) + (40 \times 57)}{100} = 45$$

However, if a single patient were considered, the corresponding *probability* of a severe stroke would be 0.60 and that of a mild stroke 0.40. Again the corresponding *expectation* of the patient's well-being score, uncertain of the severity of the stroke to be suffered, would be 0.45. 'Proportion' and 'average' are terms applied to groups and 'probability' and 'expectation' the corresponding terms applied to individuals.

There are a number of practical ways of arriving at utilities. Michael Drummond deals with these in detail in Chapter 10, and also discusses how patients' personalities can influence their preference for a gamble as opposed to a more predictable outcome.

Combining probabilities and utilities

Let us assume that we know of 100 previous patients with the same clinical features as our patient and with the same level of blood pressure on admission to hospital, and that 80 of them still had moderate persistent hypertension when the blood pressure was measured repeatedly over the ensuing four weeks (they were followed for only four weeks). It would be inferred that the probability of our patient having persistent moderate chronic hypertension was 0.80. Let us also assume that we know of another 100 previous patients with moderate chronic

hypertension who had been followed up for five years, of whom 30%
suffered a stroke during this time.

If we assume that the risk of a stroke due to moderate hypertension
is statistically independent of the risks associated with having had a
TIA, then of 100 patients admitted to hospital with these features
$(80 \times 30)/100$ will be expected to suffer a stroke within five years;
alternatively, the probability applied to our particular patient would
have been $(0.80 \times 0.30) = 0.24$.

This relationship of *statistical independence* between these groups of
patients is shown in Fig. 1a. The relationship is different in the case of

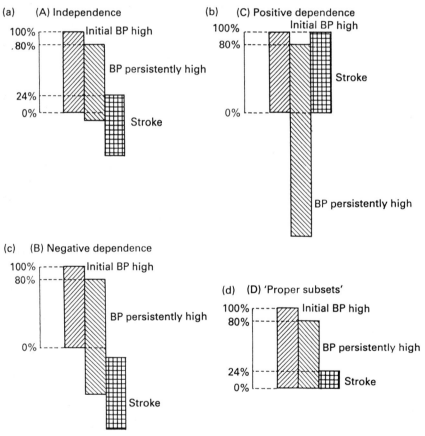

Fig. 1. *A Venn line diagram to show the possible relationships between groups of
patients with (i) high initial blood pressures, (ii) persistently high blood pressures,
and (iii) those who later suffer strokes.* Note that in all cases, 80% of those with
initial hypertension are found to have persistent hypertension, and that 30%
of the latter have strokes. However, in A and D, $(80 \times 30)\% = 24\%$ of those
with initial hypertension eventually have strokes, whereas in B none of those
with initial hypertension get strokes, and in C, 100% of those with initial
hypertension get strokes.

Fig. 1b which illustrates *negative dependence*. In this clinically unlikely situation, there are no patients with a high initial blood pressure who later suffer a stroke, despite the fact that 80% of those with a high initial blood pressure have persistent hypertension and 30% of the latter have a stroke. The latter relationship also exists for the group of patients in Fig. 1c, but here all those with a high blood pressure initially have a stroke later.

Another situation in which it is valid to multiply probabilities is when only patients with persistent hypertension who are already known to have a high initial blood pressure are considered. This situation is illustrated in Fig. 1d. In this case, the group of patients with a stroke all had previously persistently high blood pressures, and all the latter had high initial blood pressures. Thus, those with a stroke are a proper subset of those with persistently high blood pressure, and those with persistent hypertension a proper subset of those with a high initial blood pressure.

The assumption of independence is often made when probabilities are multiplied together, but it is clear from the above discussion that this should not be done without carefully considering what exactly is being assumed. In this particular situation, it would be inappropriate to make the assumption of independence because the features of a TIA make the risk of a subsequent stroke much higher. It would be better to estimate the frequency of stroke in those presenting with *all* the patient's clinical features (ie by using the 'proper subset' approach in Fig. 1d) and not by multiplying probabilities inappropriately. This is the approach taken in arriving at the probabilities and utilities used in Chapter 7. The assumption of independence is used frequently through-out probability and statistics. It is also used, for example, when calculating probabilities using Bayes' theorem (Chapter 4).

Probabilities are also multiplied with utilities in decision analysis. The point has already been made that an average utility for a group of identical patients is the same as the expected utility for an individual patient in that group. A basic principle of decision analysis is that the best decision is the one with the greatest expected (or average) utility. The method used in decision analysis is to multiply the utility of each of the possible outcomes by the probability of that outcome to obtain a 'weighted utility', and then to add all these weighted utilities together. The final result is called the 'expected utility' for that decision.

The idea of a utility can be regarded as a probability (ie in the above example, the probability which the patient chose of avoiding death to live a normal life, in order to create a reasonable gamble which the patient thought was equivalent in terms of probable well-being to living the life of a stroke victim).

On page 34 the example was chosen that the probability of the patient suffering a stroke was $(0.80 \times 0.30) = 0.24$. Let us now assume that the level of disability and distress is independent of whether the patient had previously experienced a TIA or was previously hypertensive (ie patients with a past medical history of a TIA and hypertension do not suffer more or less severe strokes than those without such a past history). The probability of having a stroke (0.24) can then be multiplied by the utility or value that the patient assigns to the post-stroke state (0.40, as specified on page 33). The product, 0.096, is a weighted utility with respect to the possible outcome of suffering a stroke. It is entered in the top branch of the decision tree shown in Fig. 2. In this context, it is just one step in the calculation of the expected utility of the decision not to treat or follow up the patient.

Decision trees

Decision trees are used to structure a clinical problem during a clinical decision analysis. The tree in Fig. 2 sets out the problem of deciding whether or not a patient with high blood pressure at first presentation should be followed up and, if necessary, treated. In practice, this would always be planned. Indeed, in the case history at the beginning of this chapter the patient was followed up and the blood pressure was found to be high (Fig. 2, branch C). However, this simple example is used to make it easier to understand the clinical decision analysis process. To analyse this decision, all the possible outcomes must also be considered.

A decision not to follow up and not to treat is represented by branches A and B of the tree shown in Fig. 2. The outcome of not following up patients can be broken down into those whose blood pressure would have been found to be persistently high (branch A) and those where it would not (branch B). In each case, the ultimate outcome on this tree is that the patient may suffer a stroke or not suffer a stroke. The same outcomes are also considered for the group of patients where a decision would be made to follow up and treat (branches C and D).

The probabilities of suffering a stroke and the associated utilities which are represented on the top branch (A) of Fig. 2 apply to a patient whose blood pressure would be persistently high but who would not be followed up and treated. The four weighted utilities for branches A and B are shown in the top panel on the right-hand side of Fig. 2. These four weighted utilities are added to provide the expected utility for the decision not to treat. This expected utility (0.770) is the same as the average value or utility for a group of patients for whom a decision has

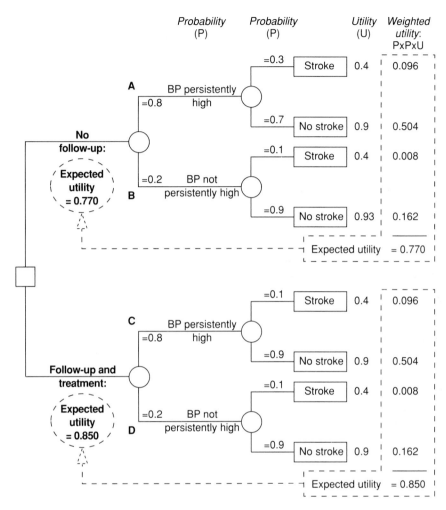

Fig. 2. *A decision tree for deciding between follow up and treatment of a high blood pressure on initial measurement, and no follow up.*

been made not to follow up and treat. To decide the best option, the entire exercise must be repeated for the group who *would* be followed up and treated (ie those represented by branches C and D). For this group, the expected utility is 0.850, which is the expected value for the decision *to* follow up and treat.

Expected utilities or expected values are easy to understand as average utilities or average values for a group of patients. However, they are often thought of as scores without a special meaning in themselves, produced during clinical decision analysis for *comparative* purposes. The decision analyst is mainly interested in the rank of the expected utility and, in particular, which is the highest. Thus, if the expected value is higher for follow up and treatment (eg 0.850 as opposed to 0.770 for no follow up and no treatment), follow up and treatment would be the best option.

In this particular example, the probabilities and utilities have been estimated subjectively but, it is important to note, explicitly. The reasoning process is also made explicit by using a decision tree and calculating the expected utilities. By making the process explicit, it becomes possible to debate the underlying assumptions. However, the scientific way of settling a contentious issue is to carry out a study which involves measuring the corresponding frequencies and utilities in an appropriate population. It is helpful for this reason to think of probabilities, utilities and expected utilities applied to an individual as being based on observed proportions, outcome measurements and averages of such measurements made on groups of *identical* patients. Decision analysis can then be regarded as a method which makes it easier to apply scientific principles to medical practice. The aim of scientific clinical medicine should be that all probabilities are based on observed frequencies (or frequency distributions — see Chapter 5) of different outcomes.

This example of decision analysis is very simple, its purpose being merely to introduce basic concepts, some knowledge of which is assumed in later chapters of this book. Furthermore, 'stroke' is an unsatisfactory diagnosis. In practice, the diagnostic possibilities must be considered in more detail, ie the patient might have suffered a cerebral infarction, cerebral haemorrhage, and so on. The various treatment options must also be considered. All this is discussed in detail in Chapter 7.

References

1. The Boston Area Anticoagulation Trial for Atrial Fibrillation Investigators. The effect of low-dose warfarin on the risk of stroke in patients with non-rheumatic atrial fibrillation. *New England Journal of Medicine* 1990; **323**: 1235–43
2. Antiplatelet Trialists' Collaboration. Secondary prevention of vascular disease by prolonged antiplatelet treatment. *British Medical Journal* 1988; **296**: 320–31
3. Thornton JG, Lilford RJ, Johnson N. Decision analysis in medicine. *British Medical Journal* 1992; **304**: 1099–2103
4. von Neumann J, Morgenstern O. *Theory of games and economic behavior.* Princeton, NJ: Princeton University Press, 1944

4 | The role of Bayes' theorem in diagnosis, prediction and decision making

Robin Knill-Jones*

The diagnosis of illness has long been regarded as an essential component of the art of medicine, even when advancing technology provides an increasing amount of the evidence needed to arrive at a decision. There are at least two components to this art: first, the knowledge gained by experience and training, which helps formulate the questions asked of a patient and the procedures used to help elucidate the patient's problem. Secondly, this experience is used in the interpretation of the evidence—obtained from whatever source. It is the interpretation of the evidence which for many is an important part of the art of medicine, a process which includes the implicit assessment of the chance or *probability* of a diagnosis or outcome. In legal terminology, the process is the *weighing of evidence*. But what is the scientific basis of interpretation? To the statistician, it is the application of an appropriate method of statistical inference that combines evidence from past experience with the findings about an individual patient. To the decision analyst, it is the combination of probabilities and various measures of outcome, which may include information about a particular patient, and which leads to the 'best decision' for an individual or a population of similar patients. The health economist sees all this, combined with some notion of cost or benefit when possible, and usually aggregates the results to arrive at the best policy for a population of patients.

The term *clinical judgement* is often applied to the whole process of medical decision making. It is more than just the weighing of evidence and assessment of uncertainty. It includes also some notion of the *value* of an outcome of an intervention, not just its probability.

How can these approaches help a clinician make a better decision for an individual patient? The time is certainly right for a careful re-examination of the diagnostic process. The relevance of this is increased by the influence of the government's White Paper, *Working for patients*,

Department of Public Health, University of Glasgow.

the acceptance of clinical audit looking at outcome, the increasing availability of resource and financial information about both procedures and diagnoses, and the concept of money following patients referred from fund-holding general practitioners.

This chapter introduces again the simple underlying principles of a formal approach to diagnosis.[1,2]

Logical diagnosis

Diagnosis would be much easier if there was no biological variability. It would then be simply a matter of *logical inference*. If patients with a specific cerebrovascular lesion always presented with the same symptoms, given those symptoms, the diagnosis would follow inevitably. The symptoms would be *sufficient* (and *necessary*) for the diagnosis. Reality is of course different. First, the same symptoms may occur as a result of a second, different disease. In this case, there is only a differential diagnosis, albeit useful if it excludes many other possibilities. The symptoms are now merely *necessary* for both diagnoses, but *sufficient* for neither. If a computerised tomography (CT) scan is capable of *always* identifying a particular lesion in one of the diseases, the presence of this lesion is also *necessary* for that disease. If it is also known that this lesion is accurately recorded without any observer variation (a most unlikely event), and is not caused by another disease process, the CT finding alone is *sufficient* for the diagnosis; in other words, no further information is needed before making the diagnosis.

The patient described in Chapter 3 has a symptom complex that fits the definition of a transient ischaemic attack (TIA). The symptom complex is *necessary* for the diagnosis. Also *necessary* are the absence of symptoms or time relationships for migraine and focal seizures. The absence of blood glucose abnormalities makes a metabolic cause for the presentation unlikely, and her age makes a non-organic or psychological cause also most unlikely. The reader will note that the notion of *probability* has now crept into the diagnostic process. It is impossible to be absolutely *certain* that the patient has had a TIA, but this is by far the most likely explanation of her presentation. It should also be noted that TIA is *not* a disease in the usual sense of the term, but merely a descriptive noun applied to a group of patients with symptoms which fit the definition, and who do not have any of the *necessary* positive findings which would indicate one diagnosis in the list of differential diagnoses. The description fits a large group of patients—it is common—and describes a clinical problem. Having carefully defined the problem, the further treatment, prognosis, and management of this group can now be improved by scientific investigation. Of course, it is likely that the cause of a TIA may eventually be found to be due to one of a number of underlying disease processes, for example, embolisation of an atheromatous plaque from an internal carotid artery, but the term itself should always be used as a description.

Statistical diagnosis

Bayes' theorem

Strictly logical diagnosis is not often possible in medicine. Much of the time the process of diagnosis is about the *implicit* use of probability by the clinician. The statistician aims to make this process *explicit*, implying a change from years of established medical practice. This has sometimes seemed threatening but, in the current climate, influenced by the lessons learned from the widely accepted process of clinical audit, the shift from an implicit to an explicit process now seems much less difficult to accept.

The use of probability can easily be illustrated in the context of a pack of cards. (The experienced reader can skip to the next section.) If all the clubs and spades and three of the low value hearts are removed, 23 cards remain. What is the probability of drawing a heart from the remaining cards? There are now ten hearts left, and the probability must be $10/23 = 0.43$. This is an unconditional probability (P) which we call P(hearts). Another example is the probability of drawing a high value card (ace, king, queen, knave). There are eight (hearts and diamonds), so the probability is $8/23 = 0.35$. This we call P(high).

If a card is now drawn and it is a heart, what is the probability that it is a high value card? Since there are only ten hearts in the modified pack, the answer is of course $4/10 = 0.40$. This is a *conditional probability*, the probability of a high card in my hand *given* that I have said that it is a heart. The usual notation is P(high|hearts), where the upright stroke '|' denotes *given*.

If another card is drawn and it is a high card, the probability that it is a heart is $4/8 = 0.50$. The denominator is different, the notation is now *reversed*, and is P(hearts|high). If 'hearts' is now regarded as a diagnosis, this is exactly what is needed to estimate the probability of a diagnosis. The example of a conditional probability given in the preceding paragraph is equivalent to the kind of information normally seen in textbooks, the probability of a symptom *given* a diagnosis. In the language of a screening test, the probability of a positive test (or symptom) *given* a diagnosis is *sensitivity* (a term to which I will return).

The second example, in which the expression is reversed, P(hearts|high), is the same as is needed from a good diagnostician: the probability of a diagnosis *given* a symptom. The sense of the *reversal* is contained in the use of the term *posterior probability* for the calculated probability of a disease.

Bayes' theorem shows how to calculate P(hearts|high) from the two unconditional probabilities and the conditional probability:

$$P(hearts|high) = P(high|hearts) \{P(hearts)/P(high)\}$$
$$= 4/10\{(10/23)/(8/23)\}$$
$$= \mathbf{0.50} \text{ (as before)}$$

For convenience, the posterior probabilities calculated in this way by the use of Bayes' theorem, or its equivalent, will be shown in **bold**.

The clinical equivalent is the calculation of the probability of a diagnosis once the prevalence of the following is known:

- the diagnosis P(hearts) in the clinic patients;
- the symptom in all the patients seen P(high); and
- the symptom in a subpopulation of patients with the diagnosis P(high|hearts). This piece of information is also called sensitivity.

There is one difference between the card example and a real patient population. In the former, there are true probabilities as there is the *total population* of cards. In the clinical setting, the total population of patients with a disease does not normally pass through a single pair of hands. Therefore, only our (limited) experience can be used to *estimate* what the long-run probabilities might be if there was access to the notional total population of patients. The more patients seen, the better the estimate. The reader will no doubt be familiar with the idea that the larger the sample, the narrower the band of the 95% confidence limits around an estimate of prevalence or, in the context of this chapter, a probability.

Combining evidence

The example given so far uses just one piece of evidence, but almost all clinical decisions are made from several pieces of evidence. The only exception is the evaluation and use of a screening test in a clinical setting or, more often, in a public health context. Clearly, any statistical method of inference needs to be able to combine evidence from a number of sources. The physician will wish to know how to combine knowledge about probabilities of several symptoms in a disease in such a way as to reflect the findings of a particular patient. The talk is of probabilities, so the instinctive method is *multiplication*—which is exactly what has to be done.

The next example uses data from the Medical Research Council European Carotid Surgery Trial.[3] The clinical setting of the example is the diagnosis of the presence of either severe or mild carotid stenosis from a few pieces of clinical information. For simplicity, the intermediate stenosis group is imagined not to exist.

Table 1 shows the prevalence of three pieces of clinical information in the two diagnostic groups expressed as probabilities, using an obvious notation P(Sym|Dis). In most published tables these would be expressed as percentages, as in Table 5 of the published paper.[3] The diagnostic problem is to estimate the probability of severe carotid stenosis from these three pieces of evidence. It has to be assumed that there are only two possible diagnoses and that they are mutually exclusive: that is, a patient can have only one of them. If that is so, the first column represents *sensitivity* of a screening test (here a symptom). The second column is about findings in patients without severe stenosis (but in fact with mild stenosis), and is related to *specificity* (in fact, it is 1.0 − specificity).

Table 1. Baseline characteristics of randomised patients.

Symptom	Severe stenosis Probability P(Sym|Dis)	Mild stenosis Probability P(Sym|Dis)
Previous		
— TIA/amaurosis fugax	0.78	0.59
— MI	0.27	0.13
Smoker	0.56	0.55

Dis = disease
Sym = symptom
MI = myocardial infarction
TIA = transient ischaemic attack

It is obvious that a patient having all three findings would be more likely to have severe stenosis than mild stenosis, since simple inspection of the table shows that in each case the findings are more common in the severe group. The statistical question is *how* much more likely? Multiplication has already been suggested as the key, and the simplest procedure is to multiply the figures in each column. Thus, $(0.78 \times 0.27 \times 0.56) = 0.118$, and $(0.59 \times 0.13 \times 0.55) = 0.042$. The value for severe stenosis is the higher—indeed, it is nearly three times more likely $(0.118/0.042)$. This ratio might be all that the decision maker seems to need, but the figures calculated so far are not real probabilities. There are only two possible diagnoses, so the probability of both *must* add up to 1.0. The two figures obtained above have therefore to be *normalised* and converted to probabilities. This is easily done by adding the two

Table 2. Probability of type of stenosis given all three baseline characteristics.

Symptom	Severe stenosis Probability		Mild stenosis Probability	
	P(Sym|Dis)	P(not Sym|Dis)	P(Sym|Dis)	P(not Sym|Dis)
Previous				
— TIA/amaurosis fugax	0.78	0.22	0.59	0.41
— MI	0.27	0.73	0.13	0.87
Smoker	0.56	0.44	0.55	0.45
Multiplication (sum = 0.160)	*0.118*		*0.042*	
P(Dis|Sym) = probability of disease given symptoms	**0.74**		**0.26**	

Dis = disease
Sym = symptom
MI = myocardial infarction
TIA = transient ischaemic attack

figures $(0.118 + 0.042) = 0.160$, and dividing each by the sum obtained (0.160). The probability of severe stenosis is now **0.74** $(0.118/0.160)$ and the probability of mild stenosis is **0.26** $(0.042/0.160)$. The ratio, of course, is nearly three (as before) (**0.74/0.26**). The results are added in to make Table 2.

The technical name for this method is the *maximum likelihood procedure* since only the P(Sym|Dis) has been used and no other information. It assumes that nothing is known about the *prevalence* of a disease in the population studied or, more precisely, it assumes that all diseases are equally likely. It should not be confused with the likelihood ratio described below.

Table 2 has columns added to represent the probability that a finding is *absent* in each category of stenosis: if 27% of patients have a history of a myocardial infarction, the remaining patients do not, and this probability is 0.73 (calculated as $1.0 - 0.27$) Thus, a patient with none of the three symptoms in the table is more likely to have mild stenosis, the probability of which, P(Dis|not Sym), may be calculated to be **0.69**.*

In the example using playing cards, one further piece of evidence was used in the calculation, namely, the underlying probability of drawing a heart in the 23 cards, P(hearts). This is equivalent to the underlying probability of disease in the total population, and can be estimated from the sample sizes used to provide the P(Sym|Dis) in Tables 1 and 2, which were 778 (severe stenosis) and 374 (mild stenosis), respectively. This extra evidence is 'free' in the sense that it might have been known *before* a new patient was seen, as in Table 1. This *prior probability* that the next patient has severe stenosis is estimated by past experience in the clinic, and is $778/(778 + 374) = 0.68$. It is easy to include this in the calculation as an extra row in the table to give Table 3. The probability of severe stenosis in the first example for a patient with all three symptoms rises from **0.74** to **0.86**. The probability of mild stenosis in a patient without the symptoms also changes, and falls from **0.69** to **0.52**. Readers who are students of racehorse form might prefer to think of the posterior probabilities as *odds*. These are calculated as $0.86/1.0 - 0.86$, or odds of about six to one on for the diagnosis of severe carotid stenosis. The inclusion of the prior probabilities of disease turns the method from the estimation of maximum likelihood to the full application of Bayes' theorem.

---

*$(0.41 \times 0.87 \times 0.45) = 0.1605$, and then normalising by $0.1605/(0.1605 + 0.0707)$ $= 0.69$.

Table 3. Probability of type of stenosis given all three baseline characteristics *and* the prior probability of disease.

	Severe stenosis Probability		Mild stenosis Probability	
	P(Sym|Dis)	P(not Sym|Dis)	P(Sym|Dis)	P(not Sym|Dis)
Prior probability	**0.68**	**0.68**	**0.32**	**0.32**
Symptom				
– TIA/amaurosis fugax	0.78	0.22	0.59	0.41
– MI	0.27	0.73	0.13	0.87
Smoker	0.56	0.44	0.55	0.45
Multiplication (sum symptoms present = 0.0937)	*0.0802*	*0.0481*	*0.0135*	*0.0514*
P(Dis|Sym) = probability of disease given symptoms and prior probabilities	**0.86**	**0.48**	**0.14**	**0.52**

Dis = disease
Sym = symptom
MI = myocardial infarction
TIA = transient ischaemic attack

Table 4. Calculation of probability of type of stenosis given all three baseline characteristics *and* the prior probability of disease, using likelihood ratios and weights of evidence.

	Severe stenosis Probability P(Sym|Dis)	Mild stenosis Probability P(Sym|Dis)	Likelihood ratios Ratio	Log
Prior probability	**0.68**	**0.32**	**2.13**	**0.327**
Symptom				
— TIA/amaurosis fugax	0.78	0.59	1.32	0.121
— MI	0.27	0.13	2.08	0.318
Smoker	0.56	0.55	1.02	0.009
Sum				**0.775**

Likelihood ratio

It now remains to describe how to move away from the laborious multiplications in the previous sections to show how the *weighing of evidence* in the clinical diagnostic process can be expressed as *weights of evidence*. These weights may simply be added up,[4] as mentioned earlier.

The process is simple to illustrate (Table 4). The likelihood ratio is P(Sym|Dis) for severe stenosis divided by the corresponding figure for mild stenosis: 0.78/0.59 = 1.32. It is clear that the bigger this ratio, the more useful the symptom as a guide to diagnosis. For example, the ratio is highest for a previous history of myocardial infarction (2.08) and lowest for smoking (1.02), since there is essentially no difference between the two diagnoses for this 'symptom'—smoking is a sort of symptom—which therefore conveys no useful information. (The ratio can also be described as sensitivity/1.0 − specificity.) The process of multiplication can be substituted by changing the ratios to their logarithms (as in the last column of Table 4) and adding them up, which gives 0.775. The individual values in the last column are called *weights of evidence*. The total can be turned back into a probability by graphical means, or by a calculation, which gives, for three symptoms, a P(Dis|3Sym) of **0.86** as before. The advantage is considerable if there are many pieces of evidence to incorporate in this way. Many practical applications multiply the weights of evidence by 10 or 100 to give a *score*, and then round up to a whole number. If 100 is used, the resulting scores are 33, 12, 32 and 1, which add to 78, for which the corresponding probability is **0.86**, again as before. The scores expressed as integers are much preferred as they are easier to read than decimals.

The independence assumption

There is an assumption in this use of Bayes' theorem, whether in its simple form, or in the *exact equivalent* which is provided by the likelihood ratios and weights of evidence. The assumption is that each symptom is statistically independent of every other within each disease (ie looking at each disease in turn). This is rarely the case in clinical medicine. In the present example, the past histories of TIA/amaurosis fugax and of myocardial infarction are likely to be associated with each other, at least in the severe stenosis group.

A more striking example is in gastroenterology: the association in patients with jaundice between them passing dark urine and having pale stools. Both are present in over 90% of patients with obstructive jaundice.[5,6] Knowing that a patient has one of these symptoms predicts with high probability a positive response to a question about the other. Obviously, the inclusion of both in a scoring system (for the diagnosis of jaundice) would lead to 'double counting'. If the assumption of independence between symptoms is broken too often, the double counting leads to an undesirable property of $P(\text{Dis}|\text{Sym})$, namely, that the estimates of probability will be too high. For example, an estimate of **0.86** for severe stenosis might be too high. The difficulty is that this cannot be known in advance using a method like Bayes' theorem which does not 'deal' with the inevitable overestimation of posterior probabilities resulting from breaking the independence assumption (for an example of overestimation, see Ref. 7). There are methods available for 'shrinking' the scores to take account of dependency between symptoms.[8] Some are approximate and relatively easy to apply, but a more rigorous, and therefore preferred, method is outlined below.

There are several possible solutions. A clinical solution is to exclude one or more groups of symptoms which are known to be strongly correlated from the scores. A statistical solution is to 'shrink' the posterior probabilities: that is, to make them less extreme. A number of approximate methods exist, but the most popular solution is to shrink the individual scores by the use of *logistic regression*. This regression method works directly on the likelihood ratios (after conversion to logarithms) essentially by including them, rather than the $P(\text{Sym}|\text{Dis})$ or the likelihoods themselves, in the regression. The statistical process 'removes' the dependent component of the scores, leaving them smaller if they are strongly correlated, or unchanged if they are not. The disadvantage is that the method is easy to apply only if there are but two diseases under consideration at one time, as in our example (once the intermediate stenoses are excluded).

Another important practical point is to insert a correction to avoid a zero probability, which might arise if a symptom had not been observed in any of the sample of patients with a disease. (This is easily done, but see Ref. 9.)

What use is to be made of the calculated probabilities? They may help indicate a diagnosis and challenge our clinical opinion. Another use is outlined in the next section, and in detail in Chapters 2 and 7.

Algorithms and decision analysis

An algorithm is merely a flow diagram, in a medical context taken to represent a logical sequence of choices in allocating patients for a trial,[3] or in describing the sequence of complications of a disease or the process of managing a clinical problem. Many algorithms have been published. How are they combined with the approach outlined above? Much of medicine is to do with probabilities, so the simplistic use of algorithms can lead to errors because they have a logical or deterministic structure. One mistake anywhere along the algorithm's path cannot be recovered as there are normally no logical loops to return the user to a point before the error occurred and then question the choice of a particular path. Anyone who has used biological keys to identify a plant, bird or insect in the UK will be familiar with the results of an error: *never found west of the Urals*. Some of these biological keys have recently begun to include error checking procedures, but few attempt to use probabilities. If an algorithm is to be used in medicine, it needs probabilities on many, if not all, of the branches. Once this is done, and some outcome measurements are introduced to the end branches and values attached to those outcomes, *clinical decision analysis* can begin to be applied,[10] as described in Chapters 2 and 7.

Conclusion

It might be asked whether calculated probabilities are any better than the implicit ones used by clinicians when making decisions about a patient. First, there is evidence that calculated probabilities *are* better than those elicited from inexperienced clinicians.[11-13] Secondly, probabilities can be used to stratify patients for a clinical trial. Thirdly, the probabilities of disease can be used in decision analysis, in combination with outcome data, to calculate the 'best' therapeutic decision for a patient when there are competing alternatives. The methods— Bayes' theorem, likelihood ratios and logistic regression—are not intrinsically difficult to appreciate. They have been shown to be closely intertwined and also linked to the more familiar concepts of sensitivity and specificity used in the assessment of a screening test. Using them in combination is consistent with obtaining the best results for patients when there are difficult choices to make. Clinical decision analysis is concerned with obtaining the best outcome for a patient, and can be constrained to do this within limited resources.

References

1. Lindley D. *Making decisions*. London: Wiley-Interscience, 1975
2. Wulff HR. *Rational diagnosis and treatment*. Oxford: Blackwell, 1976
3. European Carotid Surgery Trialists' Collaborative Group. MRC European Carotid Surgery: interim results for symptomatic patients with severe (70–90%) or with mild (0–29%) carotid stenosis. *Lancet* 1991; **337**: 1235–43
4. Knill-Jones RP. Diagnostic systems as an aid to clinical decision making. *British Medical Journal* 1987; **295**: 1392–6
5. Knill-Jones RP, Stern RB, Girmes DH, Maxwell JD, Thompson RPH, Williams R. Use of sequential Bayesian model in diagnosis of jaundice by computer. *British Medical Journal* 1973; **i**: 530–3
6. Knill-Jones RP. The diagnosis of jaundice by the computation of probabilities. *Journal of the Royal College of Physicians of London* 1975; **9**: 205–10
7. Wellwood J, Johannessen S, Spiegelhalter DJ. How does computer-aided diagnosis improve the management of acute abdominal pain. *Annals of the Royal College of Surgeons of England* 1992; **74**: 40–6.
8. Spiegelhalter DJ, Knill-Jones RP. Statistical and knowledge-based approaches to clinical decision-support systems, with an application in gastroenterology (with discussion). *Journal of the Royal Statistical Society, Series A* 1984; **147**: 35–77
9. Spiegelhalter DJ. Statistical aids in clinical decision making. *The Statistician* 1982; **31**: 19–26
10. Knill-Jones RP, Drummond MF, Kohli H, Davies L. Economic evaluation of gastric ulcer prophylaxis in patients with arthritis receiving non-steroidal anti-inflammatory drugs. *Postgraduate Medical Journal* 1990; **60**: 639–46.
11. Adams D, Chan M, Clifford PC, *et al*. Computer aided diagnosis of acute abdominal pain: a multicentre study. *British Medical Journal* 1986; **293**: 800–4
12. Malchow-Møller A, Thomsen C, Hilden J, Matzen P, Mindeholm L, Juhl E. A decision tree for early differentiation between obstructive and non-obstructive jaundice. *Scandinavian Journal of Gastroenterology* 1988; **23**: 391–401
13. Larvin M, McMahon MJ. Apache-II score for assessment and monitoring of acute pancreatitis. *Lancet* 1989; **ii**: 201–4

5 | Analysing the discriminating power of individual symptoms, signs and test results

Maurizio Koch*, Lucio Capurso* and Huw Llewelyn†

This chapter focuses on the characteristics of symptoms, signs and test results which make them useful during the diagnostic process. In this context, a test is considered to include an item of information obtained in the history or a sign on clinical examination, as well as the results of investigations. Physicians spend much of their time interpreting such findings, and when they arrive at provisional diagnoses they may arrange more tests. The underlying statistical principles for determining the usefulness of clinical information apply equally to symptoms, signs and test results. Although more reliance is sometimes placed by patients upon the results of investigations, symptoms and signs are often more powerful in discriminating terms.

The use of formal mathematical methods in diagnosis was reviewed in the previous chapter. The same statistical characteristics are required for diagnostic information to be useful when doctors interpret the same information informally. Before describing these discriminating characteristics, the diagnostic thought process which physicians appear to use will first be reviewed.

The diagnostic process

When a patient complains of a number of symptoms and also perhaps displays some physical signs in his posture, movement and mannerisms, the physician may begin to form some ideas immediately. The differential diagnosis will not only include the most probable conditions but also dangerous possibilities which may have serious consequences should there be a delay in diagnosis. Thus, when considering someone with a transient neurological dysfunction, a transient cerebral ischaemic attack (TIA) may be the most probable diagnosis, but the

*Department of Gastroenterology, General Hospital S. Filippo Neri, Rome and †School of Medicine and Dentistry, King's College, London.

possibility of a cerebral abscess may also be considered because delay in diagnosis and prompt treatment of this condition could be fatal. When physicians begin to ask questions and then to examine the patient, they will also focus on these dangerous possibilities.

At every step during the history and physical examination, and also as the results of investigations become available, the physician, if asked, would be able to list a number of diagnostic hypotheses, each with its own probability of correctly predicting the diagnosis. This means that the probability of the presence of each disease may change as each item of information becomes available. The probability before-hand is known as the *pre-test* or *prior* probability, and afterwards the *post-test* or *posterior* probability. The aim of obtaining further information is to try to increase the probability of at least one of the diagnoses. As more information becomes available, the probability of each diagnosis is re-evaluated in the light of the latest results.

This hypothetico-deductive approach is probably used by all doctors, although many may not be consciously aware of doing so unless asked to analyse their own thought processes. It consists of the formulation of a differential diagnosis, followed by a strategy designed to obtain further information which is expected to reduce the list of major possibilities (this applies to the history, physical examination and special investigations). When further information becomes available, the prior probabilities of each differential diagnosis are re-evaluated to become posterior probabilities before going through the cycle again.

The likelihood ratio

The workings of the human mind, especially when trying to arrive at a medical diagnosis, are far from well understood. It is accepted, however, that if a finding occurs commonly in some diagnoses and rarely in others, the presence of this finding will result in the diagnoses in which it occurs commonly becoming more probable, and those in which it occurs rarely becoming less probable. It is this difference of frequency of occurrence which is looked for when assessing the discriminating power of a symptom, sign or test result.

It is important to be clear about terminology when discussing discriminating power. The term 'probably' is usually applied when predicting a diagnosis, but the term 'likely' is often used instead when predicting that a symptom will be found. Thus, if a neck bruit occurs frequently in a group of patients with carotid artery stenosis (eg in 60%), in the terminology of probability theory if an individual patient has carotid artery stenosis, he or she is 'likely' (ie 0.6) to have a bruit. On the other hand, if a bruit occurs infrequently without a stenosis (eg in 20% of a group of patients who do not have a stenosis), an individual patient belonging to this group with no stenosis is said to be 'unlikely' (ie 0.2) to have a bruit. The likelihood ratio (0.6/0.2 = 3) is a measure of discrimination because it is a measure of differences between likelihoods. The 'sensitivity' of a test is the same as the 'likelihood' of observing a positive result.

In order to explore the performance of such tests, it would help to have a mathematical model which behaves in a similar way to the human mind. Chapter 4 dealt with Bayes' theorem in some detail, but some of its important features will be reviewed again briefly here. The model may be easier to understand by talking about 'odds'. The odds of carotid artery stenosis in a particular clinical situation may be said to be 2 to 1 (or 2:1, or just 2). If the probability of the diagnosis being present (2/3) is divided by the probability of the diagnosis being absent (1/3), then (2/3 ÷ 1/3) = 2. If the odds of a diagnosis are multiplied by the likelihood ratio for a test result, the answer is equal to the new odds for the diagnosis when the test result is taken into account. Thus, if the likelihood ratio for a bruit in this situation is 3, the new odds are (2 × 3) = 6. The new post-test probability with this additional information is 6/(6+1) = 0.86. Note that the probability of a diagnosis is calculated from the odds (eg 6) by dividing the latter by the (odds + 1) (eg 6/(6 + 1) = 0.86).

The post-test probability becomes a revised pre-test probability if another test result comes along. Thus, if the next finding is a duplex ultrasound scan result with a likelihood ratio of 5, the new odds are (6 × 5) = 30 and the new post-test probability is 30/(30 + 1) = 0.97. The assumption of statistical independence (page 47) implies that if the likelihood of hearing a bruit is 0.6 and the likelihood of an ultrasound result is 0.5, the likelihood of having both together is (0.6 × 0.5) = 0.3.

Weight of evidence

Instead of multiplying likelihood ratios and odds to get the new odds after receiving a test result, the process can be simplified even further. By taking the logs of the odds and likelihood ratios, the latter can be added. The log of the likelihood ratio is called the 'weight of evidence' (see Chapter 4).[1-3] If the likelihood ratio is less than 1, the log would be negative, and the total weight of evidence would fall when it is 'added' to the prior weight of evidence. The post-test odds are obtained by finding the antilog of the total weight of evidence. The post-test probability is found by dividing the odds by the (odds + 1), as described above.

The pre-test probability

The probability that the patient has a disease before performing the 'test' (which in this context means taking a history, examining the patient or performing a special investigation) is the pre-test probability. The first pre-test probability is equal to the prevalence of the disease in the population of new patients seen by the doctor. When applied to a single patient about which nothing else is known, this prevalence is usually called the 'initial' prior or pre-test probability. It thus represents the probability of the disease based on epidemiology alone. These values are difficult to obtain and require large studies if they are to be reliable.[4,5] In practice, the prior probability is often based on a subpopulation of patients with a particular presenting complaint. In the Oxford Community Stroke Project, 195 (38%) of a population of 512 patients with transient neurological symptoms had suffered a TIA.[6] Thus, if a patient presented to a general practitioner in the Oxford area at the time of the study with transient neurological symptoms (but no other information initially), the prior probability of a TIA would have been 0.38. Similar prior probabilities could be given for the other conditions.

An item of information with a short list of differential diagnoses is helpful because it simplifies the diagnostician's task. It limits the number of of diagnoses that he or she has to bear in mind and also suggests some initial hypotheses to pursue. These items of information are often called 'leads'[7,8] or 'pivots'.[9] Instead of considering the differential diagnosis of the first feature that presents, it is a much better tactic to use the best lead and 'chase up' some of the possibilities in the list by looking for items of information likely to occur in the condition being chased but unlikely to occur in the other conditions (ideally *never* occurring). A measure of a good lead would be the proportion of patients (eg 95%) with the presenting symptoms who have, say, one of four diagnoses. Alternatively, it could be the number of diagnoses necessary to explain 95% of patients with the lead. This means that fewer possibilities have to be chased.

The diagnostic 'gold standard'

In some cases, the findings which define the diagnosis are readily available to the diagnostician. This is the finding (or findings) which determines who has a condition such as a TIA. This is a criterion which it is agreed by convention must exist to allow the clinical scientist to obtain the frequency of occurrence of each symptom, sign and test result in patients with that condition. These 'gold standard' tests are often arrived at by discussion at research meetings. They may then be used as part of entry criteria for clinical trials and other studies. They are sometimes agreed at consensus meetings specifically set up for the purpose. In the case of a carotid artery stenosis, the gold standard would be a radiological image on carotid angiography. However, in the case of a TIA, a consensus meeting might decide that the gold standard requires the resolution of the neurological deficit within 24 hours, the absence of a history of migraine and a normal computerised tomography (CT) scan. Because the gold standard by definition (and thus by an artificial circular argument) occurs in no other condition, its likelihood ratio with respect to all other conditions is $x/0$ or infinity. The resulting odds are also infinity, and the probability of the diagnosis, given that the gold standard test result has been observed, is infinity/(infinity + 1) = 1.

   In the case history in Chapter 3, not much information is given about the sequence with which the symptoms and signs came to the attention of the physician. However, the sudden onset of the transient neurological deficit and its rapid resolution, together with the other findings, would make any physician strongly suspect the diagnosis of a TIA. The resolution of the neurological deficit and a normal CT scan confirms the diagnosis, as all gold standard criteria are met. But the diagnosis of TIA as it stands is not sufficiently complete. In this sense, it is an intermediate diagnosis and represents 'a mental resting place'. One of the next tasks is to decide whether or not the patient has a carotid artery stenosis.

The indices of discrimination

The likelihood ratio conveys the overall discriminating power of a symptom, sign or test result. However, there are other indices of discrimination, including the 'relative risk', the 'odds ratio' and the 'hazard ratio'. These indices are related to others, such as the predictiveness of a positive test, sensitivity and specificity. The interrelationship between these terms and how they are derived will now be explained. How these values are arrived at from observations on a population of patients is shown in Table 1.

Sensitivity and specificity

The sensitivity of a test is the likelihood that the test will be positive when the disease is present. It has two synonyms: 'positivity in disease' and 'true positive rate'. The specificity of a test is the likelihood that the test will be negative if the disease is absent. Its two synonyms are 'negativity in health' and 'true negative rate'.

It is worth noting that sensitivity and specificity cannot convey a measure of the discriminating power of a test on their own. For example, if the sensitivity is an impressive 95% but the specificity is 5%, such a test would be of no value because the likelihood ratio would be the sensitivity divided by (1 − the specificity): $0.95/(1 − 0.05) = 1$. Similarly, if the specificity is 95% but the sensitivity is 5%, the likelihood ratio for a negative test result would be the specificity divided by (1 − the sensitivity): $0.95/(1 − 0.05) = 1$.

True and false positives and predictive values

A patient who has a positive test result, and in whom the disease is present, is called a 'true positive' patient. There are a of these in Table 1. A patient who has a negative test result, and in whom the disease is absent, is called a 'true negative', and a patient who has a negative test result, but in whom the disease is actually present, is called a 'false negative'. There are d true negatives and c false negatives in Table 1. Finally, a patient who has a positive test result, but in whom the disease is absent, is called a 'false positive' (there are b of these in Table 1).

The term 'rate' (eg false positive rate) can be added to the above four terms (see Table 1). This refers to the frequency of occurrence of the positive or negative finding in those with or without the disease (not the other way around, which is sometimes a source of confusion). The frequencies with which patients with or without a disease occur in those with positive or negative test results are the various 'predictive' values.

The relative risk

The relative risk is an index of discriminating value which is often referred to in the genetics literature. It is the ratio of the post-test probabilities of the diagnosis based on a positive and negative test result: the probability of the diagnosis when the result is positive divided by the probability of the diagnosis when the result is negative. However, if the test result is to be combined with others, it is helpful to know some of the other indices in Table 1.

The hazard ratio

The 'hazard ratio' is similar to the relative risk in that it is a ratio of two probabilities of the same phenomenon given a negative and positive test result. It differs from the relative risk because it is calculated from

Table 1. A (2 × 2) table to show the relationship between the various indices of discrimination of a test.

	Disease present	Disease absent	
Test result positive	a	b	$a + b$ (Total with test positive)
Test result negative	c	d	$c + d$ (Total with test negative)
	$a + c$ (Total with disease present)	$b + d$ (Total with disease absent)	$a + b + c + d$ (Total number of patients in population studied)

The various indices of discrimination of a test:

The true positives	a
The false positives	b
The false negatives	c
The true negatives	d

True positive rate or sensitivity	$\dfrac{a}{a + c}$	Prevalence (initial pre-test probability)	$\dfrac{a + c}{a + b + c + d}$
True negative rate or specificity	$\dfrac{d}{b + d}$	Positive likelihood ratio for a positive test	$\dfrac{a/(a + c)}{b/(b + d)}$
Positive predictiveness after a positive test (post-test probability)	$\dfrac{a}{a + b}$	Negative likelihood ratio for a negative test	$\dfrac{d/(b + d)}{c/(a + c)}$
Negative predictiveness after a negative test	$\dfrac{d}{c + d}$	The relative risk (also hazard ratio)	$\dfrac{a/(a + b)}{c/(c + d)}$
Negative predictive value of a positive test	$\dfrac{c}{c + d}$	The odds ratio (approximate relative risk)	$\dfrac{a \times d}{b \times c}$
False alarm rate (1 − positive predictiveness)	$\dfrac{b}{a + b}$	The positive odds from a positive test result	a/b
False reassurance rate (1 − negative predictiveness)	$\dfrac{c}{c + d}$	The positive odds from a negative test result	c/d

survival data or the frequency of occurrence with time of some event other than death. It is the probability of not suffering the event (eg death or a stroke) at a specified time (eg five years) given a positive test (eg the presence of a bruit) divided by the probability of the same event given a negative test (eg the absence of a bruit).

The odds ratio

If the diagnosis to be predicted occurs in a very low frequency in the population being studied, the relative risk can be estimated by dividing the odds of the disease being present if the test is positive by the odds of the disease being present if the test is negative. The same result can be obtained by multiplying the number of true positive patients by the number of true negatives in the population, and dividing the answer by the number of false negatives multiplied by the number of false positives (see Table 1). Another way of calculating the odds ratio is to multiply the likelihood ratio for the presence of the disease by the likelihood ratio for its absence, which produces a ratio higher than either of the individual likelihood ratios.

The problem is that the odds ratio is often used when the disease to be predicted occurs commonly in the population, and it is not then a valid estimate of the relative risk. In this situation, it provides an overestimate of the true relative risk. The odds ratio must therefore be interpreted with caution.

The comparative likelihood ratio

The indices of discrimination described in Tables 1–3 are based on the frequency of occurrence of a test result in those with and without a 'disease' such as 50–100% carotid artery stenosis. The specificity is

Table 2. The degree of agreement between two physicians who have listened for right-sided carotid bruits in the same 100 patients with transient ischaemic attack.

Second physician ↓	First physician		
	Bruit present	Bruit absent	Totals (for 2nd physician) ↓
Bruit present	65	12	77 (Total with bruit present according to 2nd physician)
Bruit absent	18	5	23 (Total with bruit present according to 2nd physician)
Totals → (for first physician)	83 (Total with bruit present according to first physician)	17 (Total with bruit absent according to first physician)	100 (Total number of patients in population studied)

thus based on the frequency of a negative result (eg absence of a bruit) in those without a disease (eg without 50–100% carotid stenosis). In many situations, however, the diagnostician considers a list of specified differential diagnoses instead of the group of those 'without the condition'. For example, in Table 4, patients without a 50–100% stenosis are divided into 0% and 1–49% stenosis groups. The likelihood of observing a bruit in the former is 0.05, so that the comparative likelihood ratio with respect to 50–100% stenosis is 0.60/0.05 = 12. This leads to an important point. If the broad group representing 'without the condition' is subdivided into other different conditions (in the above case, different degrees of stenosis), the comparative likelihood ratios between the different conditions may be more discrimi-

Table 3. Chance agreement between two physicians who have listened for right-sided carotid bruits in the same 100 patients with transient ischaemic attack.

	First physician		
Second physician ↓	Bruit present	Bruit absent	Totals (for 2nd physician) ↓
Bruit present	*77% of 83 = 63.9*	*77% of 17 = 13.1*	*77* (Total with bruit present according to 2nd physician)
Bruit absent	*23% of 83 = 19.1*	*23% of 17 = 3.9*	*23* (Total with bruit present according to 2nd physician)
Totals → (for first physician)	*83* (Total with bruit present according to first physician)	*17* (Total with bruit absent according to first physician)	*100* (Total number of patients in population studied)

Table 4. The likelihood of occurrence of a bruit and a positive ultrasound result in patients with normal carotid arteries, and with 1–49% and 50–100% stenosis.

	Normal carotid	Stenosis	
		1–49%	50–100%
Bruit present	0.05	0.20	0.60
Duplex ultrasound positive	0.01	0.40	0.83

nating. This demonstrates the limitation of the index of specificity and other indices which are calculated by grouping 'other conditions' together. The comparative likelihood will also be discussed in a later chapter when it is used to 'eliminate' or 'prune' a differential diagnosis. For example, the presence of a bruit makes a 0% stenosis improbable.

Confidence intervals

The indices of discrimination of a test result are based on samples of varying sizes. When the index is a proportion, such as a prevalence, sensitivity or specificity, the following common approximation to the 95% confidence intervals may be used. Thus, when N is the number of individuals in the denominator of the proportion and P is the proportion, an approximation to the 95% confidence interval would be $\pm 1.96\sqrt{P(1 - P)/N}$. This method should be avoided for small values of N, for example, when $N.P$ or $N(1 - P)$ is less than 10. Thus, Hankey and Warlow showed that a bruit occurred in 64% (P) of patients with a carotid artery stenosis of 50–100%.[10] There were 115 (N) patients in the sample, so the confidence interval was from 55–73%. For a ratio of proportions such as the likelihood ratio, the calculation of the 95% confidence intervals would be more involved. Thus, if the likelihood ratio R is:

$$\frac{a/(a + c)}{b/(b + d)}$$

the confidence intervals for R may be obtained through a logarithmic transformation in an analogous way to those for a relative risk.[11,12] Thus, the standard error of $\log R$ is:

$$SE(\log_e R) = \sqrt{\frac{1}{a} - \frac{1}{a + c} + \frac{1}{b} - \frac{1}{b + d}}$$

The quantity W is found as follows:

$$W = \log_e R - [N_{1 -\alpha/2} \times SE(\log_e R)]$$

The quantity X is then found as follows:

$$X = \log_e R + [N_{1 -\alpha/2} \times SE(\log_e R)]$$

when $N_{1 - \alpha/2}$ is the approximate value from the standard normal distribution for the $100(1/\alpha - 2)$ percentile found in standard tables. The confidence intervals for the population value of R is then found from the exponentials:

$$e^W \text{ to } e^X$$

Distributions of test results

In many cases, the result of a test is a numerical value. Since the frequency of occurrence of a single numerical value is vanishingly small, it is not possible to describe the discriminating power of a numerical test result in terms of proportions such as sensitivity and specificity. Instead, numerical values are expressed as likelihood distributions. Three hypothetical likelihood distributions are shown in Fig. 1. These are based on peak flow velocity measurements made during a Doppler ultrasound scan, the degree of stenosis being determined at angiography. The first distribution of peak flow velocity is in

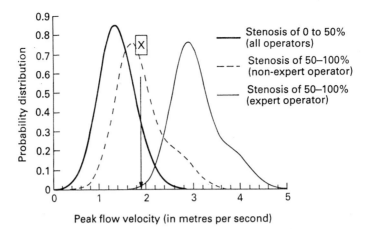

Fig. 1. *Distribution of peak flow velocity*: i) in patients without a relatively tight carotid artery stenosis; ii) in a group of patients with a relatively tight stenosis detected by an inexpert operator; iii) in the same group of patients detected by an expert operator.

patients without a relatively tight carotid artery stenosis (ie less than 50%). The second is that of the peak flow velocity as detected by an inexpert operator in a group of patients with a relatively tight stenosis (ie greater than 50%). (In patients with a relatively tight stenosis, it is not easy to identify the point at which the jet of blood is maximal, and the novice may not be able to position the measuring cursor properly to detect the point of maximum velocity.) The third distribution is that of peak flow velocity in the same group of patients but measured by an expert operator, because of which there are a greater number of high velocity readings. The first distribution has a standard Gaussian shape, but the other two are skewed to the right and also have a 'bulge'. They may be plotted by using a technique called the 'kernel method' which allows a distribution to be fitted to any data in a flexible way.[13]

At point X in Fig. 1, corresponding to a peak flow velocity of 1.9 m/sec, the number of patients in the second distribution is twice the number in the first. This means that in the hands of a non-expert observer, the likelihood of getting result X in someone with a relatively tight stenosis is twice that of getting it in a patient without a relatively tight stenosis. This means that the likelihood ratio is 2. This can be used in the calculation of a 'post-test' probability, as shown previously. Indeed, a post-test probability can be calculated for all values first being based on the measurements of the non-expert operator (Fig. 2). This is a relatively shallow curve which reflects the similarity of the distributions in the two groups of patients. If the distributions had been identical, the curve would have been a horizontal line, indicating that

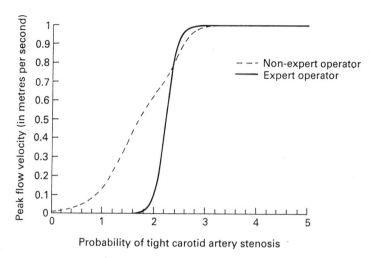

Fig. 2. *Probability of tight carotid artery stenosis*: i) based on measurements of an inexpert operator, reflecting poor discrimination between patients with and without tight stenosis; ii) based on measurements of an expert operator, reflecting good discrimination.

the probability of a relatively tight stenosis was the same for all peak flow velocity readings. However, in the case of the second curve, based on the measurements of an expert operator of the Doppler ultrasound scan, the curve is very steep. The 'perfect' curve would rise vertically from a probability of 0 to 100%. Below the point at which it rose the probability of a relatively tight stenosis would be 0, so that it would have been excluded, whereas for peak flow velocities above the point at which the curve rises, the certainty of a stenosis would be 100%.

Reproducibility and accuracy of a test result

A perfect test would be completely accurate and reproducible. Its result would be *accurate* if it provides an exact measure of the target phenomenon. In order to determine the accuracy of a test (eg hearing a bruit), its results therefore have to be compared with the result of another gold standard test (eg a Doppler ultrasound) which is assumed to be a 'correct' measure of the target phenomenon (this is of course an arbitrary assumption).

A test should be *reproducible* by producing the same result every time it is performed. Several factors affect this reproducibility:

- the patient's condition may change from time to time;
- the laboratory conditions may change;

- the test may be subject to variation in interpretation between individual observers (ie interobserver variation); and

- the test may be subject to variation in interpretation by the same observer at different times (ie intraobserver variation).

Suppose that 100 patients who had suffered a recent TIA were examined by two physicians, both of whom had listened for a bruit over the right carotid artery (see Table 2). They agreed that five of these 100 patients had no bruit, and that a further 65 had a bruit originating from the right carotid artery. In the remaining 30 cases, the two physicians did not agree. This means that they agreed with each other in 70 (5 + 65) out of 100 cases, and the interobserver agreement is therefore 70%. This is an overall measure agreement however. The proportion of times they agreed about a specific observation (in this case the bruit) is known as the specific agreement, and was 65% in the example. Intraobserver agreement (when the same physician repeats the examination) may be represented in the same way.

It is possible that two observers may agree in a high proportion of cases by chance so, in order to provide a useful measure of agreement, allowance must be made for the contribution of chance agreement. For example, if the first physician heard the bruit in 77% of cases, and the second physician in 83%, they would hear it in the same patient by chance in $(77 \times 83) = 63.9\%$ of cases. Similarly, the first physician would fail to hear the bruit in 23% of cases and the second physician in 15%, so that by chance they would fail to hear it in the same patient in 3.5% of cases. The total chance for 'hearing' and 'not hearing' the bruit in the same patient would be $(63.9 + 3.5) = 67.4\%$. The observed agreement was 70%, so the agreement over and above chance was only $(70 - 68.4) = 1.6\%$. The maximum proportion of times the physicians could have agreed was 77% (the other physician also hearing the bruit in an extra $(83 - 77) = 6\%$ of cases). Therefore, the maximum possible agreement over and above chance would be $(77 - 67.4) = 9.6\%$. The actual difference was 1.6%, the ratio of actual to maximum being $1.6/9.6 = 0.167$. This ratio is known as the kappa statistic. The kappa statistic for total agreement is 1.0, and for maximum possible disagreement, -1. Chance agreement alone is represented by a kappa statistic of 0.

Meta-analysis

If several small studies are performed on the same disease and findings yielding results of the kind shown in Table 1, it might be helpful to pool the results — particularly if different studies produce different values for the likelihood ratios, sensitivities, etc. Clearly, the results would have to be examined carefully to make sure they are of a reasonable standard. The technique of combining the different studies is known as meta-analysis,[14] and is a formal approach to the informal process of taking a broad view from several studies and from personal experience. Simply finding the average statistic (eg the average sensitivity) from a number of studies may give a misleading result. Instead, meta-analysis treats each study in a self-contained way, but the final results are combined to give an overall result.

The simplest way of combining the results of different studies was described by Woolf.[15] This method computes an overall statistic to arrive at a weighted average of the individual statistics. The example statistic used here is the sensitivity. Let us assume that a Medline search on the keywords 'epidemiological methods', 'sensitivity', 'duplex ultrasonography' and 'carotid stenosis' has come up with seven papers. Before incorporating the data from a series of papers into a meta-analysis, they should be reviewed carefully. This can be done in a quantitative way.[16] Four of these are rejected because they do not satisfy pre-defined criteria for acceptability. The data in the remaining three papers may be summarised as shown in Table 5. The weighted mean of the different sensitivities is obtained by multiplying the sensitivity from each study by the number of patients used in that study to arrive at the overall sensitivity. This gives the number of patients in each study corresponding to the $(a + c)$ cells in Table 1. The total number of patients in all the $(a + c)$ cells is then divided by the total number of patients in the $(a + c)$ cells used to arrive at the sensitivity. The calculation is shown in Table 5.

Table 5. Pooling of data during meta-analysis.

Study	No. of patients	Sensitivity
I	150	0.91
II	40	0.88
III	90	0.94
Total no. of patients	280	

Weighted mean of the sensitivity:

$(150/280 \times 0.91) + (40/280 \times 0.88) + (90/280 \times 0.94)$

$= 0.50 + 0.13 + 0.30 = 0.93$

Cochran proposed that the approach should be extended to include a random effect model which takes account of the variance between the results of studies as well as the variance within them.[17] This approach has been revised by DerSimonian and Laird.[18] There is a recent review of these methods which is accompanied by computer programmes that can perform these calculations conveniently.[19]

Reading a paper on the discriminating power of a test

When evidence in favour of the discriminating power of a test result is being published, indices such as those in Table 1 are usually presented in the results section. There may also be comparative likelihood ratios with respect to two conditions such as as TIA and cerebral tumour. In order to assess whether these indices have been arrived at in a reliable way, the following questions need to be addressed:[20,21]

1. Is the gold standard appropriate and defined carefully, and were the observers genuinely ignorant of the gold standard test result when they observed the results of the test being assessed? If they knew the diagnosis already, bias may have crept in to make them read the test result in the most favourable light.

2. Is the result of the new test to be assessed used to decide who should have the gold standard test? If so, the new test would be artificially positive in all patients with the disease. The sensitivity might be 100% if this is done consistently.

3. Does the group of patients studied possess the spectrum of severity of disease usually encountered in that clinical setting? If the test is performed on a group of individuals rarely encountered in routine clinical practice, there is a danger of exaggerating the apparent discriminating power of the test. For example, if a duplex ultrasound scan is assessed on patients with severe carotid stenosis and a group of young healthy volunteers, its apparent ability to discriminate between patients with and without carotid stenosis would be exaggerated. A group of controls of ages similar to the test patients should be used, as it is known that bruits not associated with stenosis increase with age.

4. Is the setting of the study, as well as the way in which patients were selected for referral to hospital, admission to hospital and transfer to specialist units described adequately? If these details are not clear, it would be difficult to assess the extent to which the same test can be applied in general clinical practice.

5. If the test relies heavily on human judgement, are its reproducibility (when several readings are performed several times on one patient

by one operator) and interobserver variation documented? In some cases, the originator of a test may develop an expertise which cannot be easily achieved by others. For example, the performance of some ultrasound techniques are heavily dependent on the operator's skill.

6. If the term 'normal' is applied to a test result, is it explained properly? The term may apply to two standard deviations of a normally distributed set of numerical values in a clearly defined population of patients, or to a range within the 5th and 95th centile of a population. It may be a finding which carries no additional risk of morbidity, a range of culturally or socially desirable values to which some people may aspire (eg height) or a range beyond which a patient's result is generally accepted to fall within the definition of a gold standard. In some cases, the term 'normal' is applied to the therapeutic range of a drug.

7. If the test is performed as part of a sequence of tests, is its place in the sequence stated clearly? In some cases, a test needs to be done only if the diagnosis is in doubt. For example, if a patient with a transient neurological deficit also gives a history of tongue biting, incontinence and failure to take anti-epileptic treatment regularly, it would be inappropriate to perform carotid ultrasound. To include epileptic patients in the group of those without carotid stenosis in order to get data on the diagnostic accuracy of ultrasound would be inappropriate.

8. Have the tactics for carrying out the test been described in sufficient detail to allow its replication? This applies to the test methodology and the patient's preparation, including diet, avoidance of certain drugs, etc.

9. Has the utility, and thus the contribution, of the test to the patient's overall benefit been determined?

10. Have the overall resource implications of the proposed test been taken into account?

Conclusion

Care has to be taken with the analysis of the clinical usefulness of symptoms, signs and special investigations. Many different indices of discrimination are used in different circumstances, the most informative of which is the likelihood ratio.

References

1. Good IJ. *Probability and weighing of evidence.* London: Charles Griffin, 1950
2. Kullbach S. *Information theory and statistics.* New York: John Wiley, 1979
3. Rembold CM, Watson D. Post test probability calculation by weights. *Annals of Internal Medicine* 1988; **108**: 115–20
4. Spiegelhalter DJ, Knill-Jones RP. Statistical and knowledge-based approaches to clinical decision-support systems, with an application in gastroenterology (with discussion). *Journal of the Royal Statistical Society, Series A* 1984; **147**: 35–77
5. Capurso L, Koch M, Dezi A, Koch G, Di Cocco U. Towards a quantitative diagnosis of dyspepsia: the value of clinical symptoms. The dyspepsia project report. *Italian Journal of Gastroenterology* 1988; **20**: 191–202
6. Dennis M, Bamford J, Sandercock P, Warlow C. Prognosis of transient ischaemic attacks in the Oxfordshire Community Stroke Project. *Stroke* 1990; **21**: 848–53
7. Llewelyn DEH. Mathematical analysis of the diagnostic relevance of clinical findings. *Clinical Science* 1979; **57**: 477–9
8. Llewelyn DEH. The logic of justification in medical audit. In: Capurso L, Koch M, Pola P, eds. *Informatica e Gastroenterologia.* Rome: Editore Marrapese, 1990
9. Eddy DM, Clanton CH. The art of diagnosis: solving the clinicopathological conference. *New England Journal of Medicine* 1982; **306**: 1263–8
10. Hankey GJ, Warlow CP. Symptomatic carotid ischaemic events: safest and most cost effective way of selecting patients for angiography, before carotid endarterectomy. *British Medical Journal* 1990; **300**: 1489–91
11. Katz D, Baptista J, Azen SP, Pike MC. Obtaining confidence intervals for the risk ratio in cohort studies. *Biometrics* 1978; **34**: 469–74
12. Gardener MJ, Altman GA. *Statistics with confidence: confidence intervals and statistical guidelines.* London: British Medical Journal, 1989
13. Copas JB. Plotting p against x. *Applied Statistics* 1983; **32**: 21–31
14. Glass GV. Primary, secondary and meta-analysis of research. *Education Researcher* 1976; **5**: 3–8
15. Woolf B. On estimating the relation between blood group and disease. *Annals of Human Genetics* 1955; **19**: 251–3
16. Chalmers TC, Blum A, Buyse M, Hewitt P, Koch M. *Data analysis for clinical medicine: the quantitative approach to patient care in gastroenterology.* Rome: International University Press, 1988
17. Cochran WG. The combination of estimates from different experiments. *Biometrics* 1954; **10**: 101–29
18. DerSimonian R, Laird N. Meta-analysis in clinical trials. *Controlled Clinical Trials* 1986; **7**: 157–88
19. Chalmers TC, Smith H, Blackburn B, *et al.* A method for assessing the quality of a randomised controlled trial. *Controlled Clinical Trials* 1981; **2**: 31–49
20. Philbrick JT, Horowitz RI, Feinstein AR. Methodologic problems of exercise testing for coronary artery disease: groups, analysis and bias. *American Journal of Cardiology* 1980; **46**: 807–912
21. Sackett DL, Haynes RB, Tugwell P. *Clinical epidemiology. A basic science for clinical medicine.* Boston: Little, Brown and Company, 1991

6 | A physician arriving at diagnoses, predictions and decisions

Graeme J. Hankey*, James M. Slattery* and Charles P. Warlow†

The case history outlined in Chapter 3 will be analysed in more detail in this chapter to illustrate how a clinician reasons, based upon the evidence of the published scientific literature.

The case to be discussed is a 70-year-old woman who has experienced an episode of transient focal neurological dysfunction (left brachiofacial weakness) of sudden onset, which resolved completely within 4–24 hours. She is a smoker, with evidence of non-valvular atrial fibrillation, chronic hypertension (her blood pressure is 200/120 mmHg, she has grade II hypertensive retinopathy and left ventricular hypertrophy), a bruit over the asymptomatic carotid artery, and a marginally elevated serum cholesterol.

Establishing the diagnosis

The doctor's first task is to formulate a differential diagnosis of transient focal neurological dysfunction in a 70-year-old woman (Table 1). The diagnosis of some of the disorders in Table 1 depends almost entirely upon the clinical history and cannot be confirmed or rejected by any objective laboratory test or procedure. Consequently, the doctor depends on the patient's capacity to give a clear account of the sudden onset of focal neurological dysfunction and on his or her ability to elicit and interpret the history accurately. Frequently, in practice, the clinical history is not clear, either because the onset of the symptoms was ill-defined or has been forgotten by the patient, the symptoms themselves were non-localising (eg dizziness, confusion) or have been forgotten, or they may have been remembered but are difficult to describe (eg transient hemianopia). Also, as patients are not infrequently frightened by the attack, they may become more preoccupied with the immediate outcome than with the nature of the

*Department of Clinical Neurosciences, Western General Hospital, Glasgow and †University of Clinical Neurosciences, Northern General Hospital, Edinburgh.

Table 1. Is it a transient ischaemic attack?

Transient focal neurological dysfunction: differential diagnosis

Ischaemia (TIA)

Migraine

Partial seizures

Structural intracranial lesion
—Tumour: meningioma
—Aneurysm
—Arteriovenous malformation
—Subdural/intracerebral haematoma

Metabolic
—Hypoglycaemia
—Hyponatraemia

Demyelination
—Multiple sclerosis

Peripheral nerve dysfunction
—Mononeuropathy

Psychological

TIA = transient ischaemic attack

deficit and may not present to medical attention for some time, during which many of the details of the attack have been forgotten. All these problems are particularly prevalent in the elderly, who not infrequently suffer a transient ischaemic attack (TIA). The value of an eyewitness account cannot be overestimated.

The patient under discussion experienced the abrupt onset of symptoms of focal neurological dysfunction, which were maximal at onset and without intensification and spread. The symptoms were 'negative', representing a loss of (motor) function and they resolved within 24 hours. This was almost certainly a TIA as all the features concur with a widely accepted definition of TIA: an acute loss of focal cerebral or monocular function with symptoms lasting less than 24 hours, and thought to be due to inadequate cerebral or ocular blood supply as a result of arterial thrombosis or embolism associated with arterial, cardiac or haematological disease.

The major disorders to be distinguished from TIA in this 70-year-old woman are migraine, focal seizures and a structural intracranial lesion.

Migraine

It is unlikely that this patient was suffering her first-ever episode of migraine with aura (classical migraine), because the aura of migraine is

usually characterised by positive symptoms of focal neurological dysfunction that develop gradually and 'build up' over 5–20 minutes,
lasting less than 60 minutes in total. The most common aura consists of
homonymous or central visual symptoms, such as flashes of light,
scintillations or fortification spectra, which gradually build up, expand
and migrate across the visual field. Motor (and sensory) disturbances
may occur, such as weakness in this case, but they usually evolve over a
period of minutes in a 'marching' fashion, such as from arm to facial
weakness, typically lasting less than one hour, not between four and 24
hours, as in the case history. Headache, nausea and/or photophobia
usually follow the aura.

Although this patient did not suffer a headache, the diagnosis of
migraine cannot be excluded on this basis alone. Some patients who
regularly experience migraine with aura also suffer similar episodes of
'positive' neurological dysfunction at other times but without headache. It can be quite difficult to distinguish TIA and migraine when the
patient with known migraine presents following a first-ever episode of
transient positive symptoms of focal neurological dysfunction without
associated headache, particularly if the patient is elderly and has other
vascular diseases and risk factors. The patient under discussion,
however, clearly did not have migraine; she had no past history or
family history of migraine, and suffered the sudden onset of negative
symptoms that were maximal at onset and did not build up.

Epileptic seizures

As with migraine, focal seizures usually cause positive or excessive
sensory or motor phenomena, but the onset is quite sudden and, if the
symptoms spread, they do so quite rapidly over several seconds rather
than minutes. In TIAs, negative symptoms tend to arise all at once. It
is possible that this patient had a post-ictal or Todd's paresis, but there
is no history of preceding convulsion. Although somatic inhibitory
seizures have been long recognised, it is rare for epileptic seizures to
cause transient negative symptoms during the ictal discharge. When
they do, the deficit is usually brief and does not last hours, as in this
case. It would have been difficult to exclude a seizure disorder,
however, if the patient had awoken with a hemiparesis which recovered
as the day proceeded. In these circumstances, a post-ictal paresis
following an unrecognised nocturnal seizure would have been possible.

Intracranial structural lesions

In about 1% of patients presenting with transient focal neurological
dysfunction of sudden onset, the underlying cause is a structural

intracranial lesion such as a chronic subdural haematoma, cerebral tumour or arteriovenous malformation, presumably as a result of seizure activity, ischaemia due to a vascular steal phenomenon or even a small intraparenchymal haemorrhage. With the possible exception of an arteriovenous malformation, these were excluded in this case by the normal CT scan.

Metabolic disturbances

Metabolic disturbances such as hypoglycaemia, hyponatraemia, hypercalcaemia, and hepatic and renal failure are rare causes of focal neurological symptoms. Hypoglycaemia is usually manifest by symptoms of hunger, generalised weakness and compensatory adrenergic discharge. However, hypoglycaemia may present with isolated focal neurological signs (usually a hemiparesis) which resolve following resolution of the hypoglycaemia. Although the blood glucose was normal during the deficit in the patient under discussion, this does not entirely exclude hypoglycaemia as the cause (because the blood glucose can be in the so-called 'normal' range and cause focal neurological symptoms that are corrected by glucose supplementation), but it would be very unlikely that she would have an insulinoma nor is she on any hypoglycaemic medication.

Psychological

Some patients experience recurrent attacks of transient focal or non-focal neurological dysfunction which do not have an organic basis. Emotionally-based attacks not related to misdiagnosed psychiatric illness take several forms, such as hyperventilation, panic or anxiety attacks, and deliberate simulation. These are uncommon in 70-year-old women, particularly when they occur for the first time at this age.

Interobserver variation in the diagnosis of transient ischaemic attack

Although the diagnosis of TIA is strongly suggested in this patient, it remains arguable as there is no diagnostic test. Not only do general practitioners and hospital doctors have difficulty with the diagnosis of TIA,[1] but experienced neurologists also have difficulty agreeing about it amongst themselves.[2]

Anatomy of the transient ischaemic attack

Having established the diagnosis of TIA from the clinical history, the second task is to determine which arterial territory in the brain or eye has been rendered ischaemic, particularly if carotid angiography and endarterectomy are being considered.

The patient under discussion appeared to have clinical evidence of dysfunction of only the right corticobulbar tract, somewhere between the motor cortex (pre-rolandic gyrus) of the right cerebral hemisphere (via the subcortical white matter, internal capsule and mid-brain cerebral peduncle) and the ventral pons on the right. The clinician was fortunate to be able to examine the patient before the deficit had resolved (which is unusual) and to confirm the left brachiofacial weakness. At that time, special attention would have been given to eliciting any evidence of right parietal dysfunction (visuospatial perceptual dysfunction if right-handed or language dysfunction if left-handed), right parieto-occipital dysfunction (left homonymous hemianopia) or brainstem and cerebellar dysfunction (lower cranial nerve palsies, nystagmus, ataxia, etc.). In the absence of additional signs, it is not possible to be certain of the arterial distribution of the TIA (Table 2) because the corticobulbar tract shares both carotid and vertebrobasilar blood supply at different points. Nevertheless, as only a

Table 2. What is the anatomy of the transient ischaemic attack?

Symptom	Arterial territory		
	Carotid	Either	Vertebrobasilar
Dysphasia	+		
Monocular visual loss	+		
Unilateral weakness*		+	
Unilateral sensory disturbance*		+	
Dysarthria		+	
Homonymous hemianopia		(+)	+
Unsteadiness/ataxia		(+)	+
Dysphagia		(+)	+
Diplopia**			+
Vertigo**			+
Bilateral simultaneous visual loss			+
Bilateral simultaneous weakness			+
Bilateral simultaneous sensory disturbance			+
Crossed sensory/motor loss			+

TIA = transient ischaemic attack
*usually regarded as carotid distribution.
**NOT if sole symptom, only if associated with one or more other symptom on list.

part of the arm and face was paralysed, and not the whole arm and face, it is much more likely that the right motor cortex and/or adjacent subcortical region was ischaemic, manifesting as a cortical TIA in the territory of the right internal carotid artery. If the patient had experienced one of the lacunar syndromes such as an isolated weakness and/or sensory disturbance in all the face and arm, or arm and leg, or face, arm and leg or, indeed, an ataxic hemiparesis (dysarthria — clumsy hand syndrome), this would be classified as a lacunar TIA, which is usually due to intracerebral small penetrating artery disease.[3]

The cause of the transient ischaemic attack

In order to predict outcome and implement appropriate treatment, the third task is to establish the likely cause of the TIA.

The history and examination findings usually provide several clues to the likely cause of the TIA (Table 3). In the patient under discussion, the most likely cause is atherothromboembolism from the extracranial carotid artery or cardiogenic embolism from the left atrium.

Table 3. What is the cause of the transient ischaemic attack?

Cause	%
Arterial (thromboembolism/low flow)	75
Atheroma (large extracranial arteries)	40
Atheroma (large intracranial arteries)	10
Lipohyalinosis/microatheroma (small intracranial arteries)	20
Arteritis	<5
Dissection	<1
Cardiac (embolism)	20
Valvular heart disease	
Cardiomyopathy/ischaemic heart disease	
Haematological (thromboembolism)	<5
Hyperviscosity	
Coagulopathy	

The hypothetical patient has several risk factors for atherosclerosis: advanced age, hypertension, cigarette smoking and borderline hypercholesterolaemia. These are not uncommon in TIA patients, the exact frequencies varying because of referral bias in different cohorts and different strategies of investigation. The patient also has a carotid bruit on the asymptomatic side (which suggests more widespread atheromatous arterial disease), but it is not stated whether she has symptoms or signs of coronary or peripheral vascular insufficiency. The initial blood pressure recording of 200/120 mmHg probably reflected an acute stress response to some extent, but not completely. Subsequent recordings on days 3 and 14 revealed a persistently elevated blood pressure (170/105 mmHg), consistent with other evidence of end-organ damage due to chronic hypertension—the retinopathy and left ventricular hypertrophy. Although the presence of a high cervical arterial bruit is suggestive of internal carotid stenosis, it is not a sufficiently accurate predictor upon which to base further management. Bruits may be found over both normal and occluded arteries (Fig. 1). Such bruits may be due to stenosis of the external carotid artery, for example.[4]

As non-valvular atrial fibrillation is associated with about 45% of cerebral emboli that are presumed to be of cardiac origin,[5] the presence of atrial fibrillation in this patient raises the possibility of a cardiac source of cerebral embolism accounting for the TIA. The type of cerebral ischaemic deficit in this patient (probably cortical TIA, as opposed to lacunar TIA) is consistent with middle cerebral branch artery occlusion by an embolus originating in either the heart or the proximal larger arteries. The possible mechanisms of cerebral ischaemia in patients with atrial fibrillation include emboli due to stasis-related left atrial thrombi from structural abnormalities of the mitral value (thickening, myxomatous degeneration, annular calcification), and from stasis-related left ventricular thrombi, and thromboembolism associated with other co-existing pathologies such as atherosclerotic coronary artery and haematological diseases. Echocardiography is reported to have shown no valvular disease and no atrial thrombus. It is important to know whether this was a transthoracic two-dimensional or a trans-oesophageal echocardiograph, because the former does not give a good image of the left atrium and left atrial appendage. Nevertheless, a normal study does not exclude a cardiac source of embolism (because a left atrial clot may be too small or have already embolised), and a positive echocardiogram (visualised thrombus) does not confirm cardiogenic embolism (because the thrombus may not have embolised).

In this patient, it is likely that the ischaemic symptoms are due to embolic occlusion of a branch of the upper division of the right middle cerebral artery, but it is impossible to determine whether the source of the embolus was the internal carotid artery (extracranial or intracranial), the heart or proximal arterial circulation (or indeed possibly the venous circulation via a patent right to left cardiopulmonary shunt).

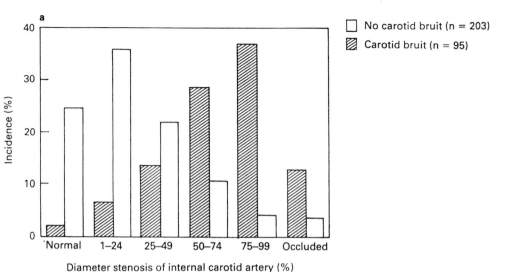

Fig. 1(a). *Range of diameter stenosis of internal carotid artery on the symptomatic side in transient ischaemic attack and retinal infarction patients with (n = 95) and without (n = 203) a carotid bruit.* (Reproduced from Ref. 4 by permission of the *British Medical Journal.*)

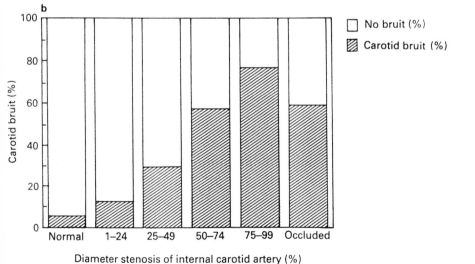

Fig. 1(b). *Relative proportion of ipsilateral carotid bruit or no bruit for each stratum of diameter stenosis of the internal carotid artery on the symptomatic side (n = 298).* (Reproduced from Ref. 4 by permission of the *British Medical Journal.*)

What is the risk of stroke and other vascular events?

For patients with TIA referred to hospital, like this patient, the average annual risk of stroke (Fig. 2) is about 3.4% (95% CI: 2.5–4.6%).[6] However, the importance of TIAs is not only that they indicate an increased risk of stroke but also an increased risk of other serious vascular events. The average annual risk of a coronary event, which is the most common cause of death in patients with TIA, is about 3.1% (95% CI: 2.2–4.0%), and the average annual risk of the composite outcome event stroke, myocardial infarction or vascular death is about 6.5% (95% CI: 5.3–7.8%) (Fig. 2).[6,7]

The above figures reflect the average prognosis for a large cohort (or group) of patients with TIA, but within each cohort there is tremendous variation in the outcome of individual patients with TIA; some do well, while others do poorly. The prognosis of patients with TIA depends heavily on the presence or level of prognostic factors among them. The significant adverse prognostic factors have recently been identified in one cohort of 469 patients with TIA for (i) stroke, (ii) coronary event and (iii) stroke, myocardial infarction or vascular death (Table 4). Using these factors and their associated hazard ratios, predictive equations have been formulated both of relative risk (Table 4) and of absolute risk (Table 5).[8] According to this model, the patient whose history is described in Chapter 3 has an absolute risk of stroke of 8% in the first year and 24% after five years, of a coronary event, 1% in the first year and 9% after five years, and of stroke, myocardial infarction or vascular death, 8% in the first year and 31% after five years.

How to treat the patient

Strategies of secondary prevention of serious vascular events are aimed at reducing the risk of such events, and are based, first, on reducing or ameliorating the modifiable causes or risk factors and, secondly, on implementing antithrombotic treatment and carotid surgery in appropriate patients.

What are the risk factors?

Age and male sex are two risk factors that have a high population attributable risk of stroke but which cannot be modified. The most important modifiable risk factors for ischaemic stroke (and also coronary events) are hypertension, cigarette smoking and hypercholesterolaemia, all of which applied to the patient under discussion.

(a)

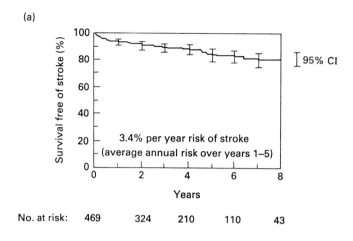

No. at risk: 469   324   210   110   43

(b)

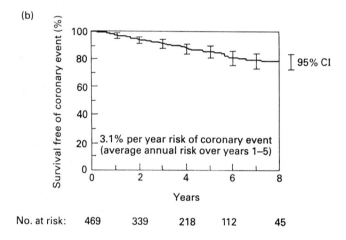

No. at risk: 469   339   218   112   45

(c)

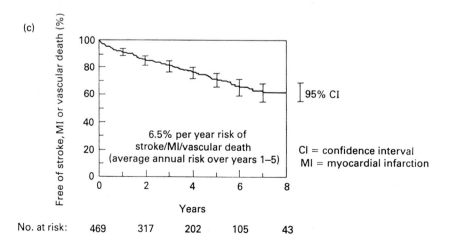

No. at risk: 469   317   202   105   43

Blood pressure

For people with a diastolic blood pressure in the range 70–110 mmHg, a decrease in diastolic blood pressure of 7.5 mmHg for 2–3 years should be associated with a reduction of stroke risk by half and coronary event risk by nearly one-third.[9,10] The proportional reduction in stroke associated with reducing blood pressure is similar in high- and low-risk individuals, so the size of any absolute reduction in stroke incidence (produced by reducing blood pressure) depends on the absolute risk (or incidence) of stroke. This patient has a relatively high risk of stroke (about 8% in the first year), and therefore a lot to gain potentially if it could be halved to about 4% in the first year.

How to treat blood pressure. A large number of non-pharmacological and pharmacological treatments are now available for the management of hypertension. One of the major problems is maintaining patients consistently on long-term therapy, so these treatments must be applied individually to enhance long-term compliance, and therefore benefit, and minimise potential harm for what is often a lifelong disorder. In order to accomplish this goal, a thorough understanding is needed of important characteristics both of the individual patient and of the available therapeutic modalities.[11,12]

Non-pharmacological therapy. Several non-drug interventions may decrease blood pressure and either eliminate the need for drug therapy in patients with mild hypertension or complement drug therapy in more severely hypertensive patients (Table 6). These interventions may not decrease blood pressure in all patients, and it cannot be predicted beforehand which patients will respond. However, as they cause little or no harm, and may provide other health benefits in addition to their blood pressure-lowering effect, they should be recommended to all people, not only patients, if appropriate.

The initial step in the treatment of this patient's hypertension is to identify potential non-pharmacological therapeutic modalities that may be helpful (Table 6). Depending on the dietary history, these may include modification of the intake of salt,[13–15] calories,[16–18] and

Fig. 2. *Kaplan-Meier survival curves showing the percentage survival free of (a) stroke, (b) coronary event, and (c) stroke, myocardial infarction or vascular death (censoring those dying from causes other than (a) stroke, (b) coronary event, and (c) stroke, myocardial infarction or vascular death, respectively) during the first eight years after a transient ischaemic attack. The vertical error bars are the 95% confidence intervals of the estimate (adapted from Hankey et al.[6]).*

Table 4. Prediction models for relative risk of each outcome event derived from stepwise Cox proportional hazards multiple regression analysis of survival data of 469 patients with transient ischaemic attack (data from Hankey et al.[8]). (Selection criteria: variables entered if $p < 0.03$ and removed if $p > 0.05$.)

Factor	Beta coefficient	p-value	Hazard ratio	Hazard ratio 95% Confidence interval
Stroke, myocardial infarction or vascular death (n = 118 events)				
Age	0.06	<0.001	**1.06 (1.82)**	1.04–1.09
Peripheral vascular disease	0.84	<0.001	**2.31**	1.52–3.50
No. of TIAs in last 3 months	0.02	<0.001	**1.02 (1.16)**	1.01–1.02
Male sex	0.68	0.002	**1.98**	1.27–3.07
Carotid and VB TIAs	0.71	0.008	**2.03**	1.20–3.43
TIA brain (vs. AFx only)	0.56	0.019	**1.75**	1.10–2.78
Left ventricular hypertrophy*	0.54	0.026	**1.72**	1.07–2.76
Residual signs	0.66	0.044	**1.93**	1.02–3.65
No additional variables selected using the less stringent criteria: enter if $p < 0.10$ *and remove if* $p > 0.15$				
Stroke (n = 63 events)				
Model with significant prognostic variables for stroke, MI or vascular death forced in				
No. of TIAs in last 3 months	0.02	0.001	**1.02 (1.17)**	1.01–1.03
Age	0.05	0.003	**1.05 (1.57)**	1.03–1.08
Peripheral vascular disease	0.76	0.010	**2.13**	1.20–3.80
Left ventricular hypertrophy*	0.68	0.035	**1.98**	1.05–3.72
TIA brain (vs. AFx only)	0.72	0.038	**2.05**	1.04–4.03
Residual signs	0.74	0.072	**2.09**	0.94–4.69
Carotid and VB TIAs	0.53	0.151	**1.69**	0.82–3.48
Male sex	0.36	0.217	**1.43**	0.81–2.54
Additional variables selected using the less stringent criteria: enter if $p < 0.10$ *and remove if* $p > 0.15$				
Ischaemic heart disease				
Carotid bruit				

(Table 4 continued)

Coronary event (*n* = 58 events)
Model with significant prognostic variables for stroke, MI or vascular death forced in

Age	0.08	<0.001	**1.08 (2.25)**	1.05–1.12
Ischaemic heart disease*	0.87	0.002	**2.39**	1.37–4.18
Male sex	1.02	0.003	**2.77**	1.40–5.50
Carotid and VB TIAs	1.07	0.004	**2.91**	1.41–5.99
Peripheral vascular disease	0.59	0.063	**1.81**	0.97–3.39
No. of TIAs in last 3 months	0.01	0.117	**1.01 (1.10)**	0.998–1.02
TIA brain (vs. AFx only)	0.44	0.180	**1.55**	0.82–2.95
Residual signs	0.48	0.339	**1.62**	0.60–4.31
Left ventricular hypertrophy	0.33	0.347	**1.39**	0.70–2.78

No additional variables selected using the less stringent criteria: enter if p <0.10 *and remove if* p >0.15

AFx = amaurosis fugax
MI = myocardial infarction
TIA = transient ischaemic attack
VB = vertebrobasilar

*Additional prognostic variables selected using stepwise procedure (enter if *p* <0.03, remove if *p* >0.05) after the significant variables had been forced into the model.

Hazard ratios of continuous variables, such as age and no. of TIAs, have also been estimated in bracketts above (eg for every 10 TIAs in the last 3 months the hazard ratio for stroke increases by a factor of 1.17; for an increase in age of one decade, the hazard ratio for stroke increases by a factor of 1.57).

Table 5. Prediction equations (data from Hankey et al.[8]).

Prediction equation for survival free of stroke, myocardial infarction or vascular death

Indicate if applicable to this patient	Start			Cumulative score
**	(Age−60)	Multiplied by	6	60
	Female	Subtract	68	−8
	Amaurosis fugax only	Subtract	56	
	Carotid and vertebrobasilar TIAs	Add	71	
	More than one TIA in last 3 months	Add	$(1.5 \times [n - 1])$	
	Peripheral vascular disease	Add	84	
	Residual neurological signs	Add	66	
**	Left ventricular hypertrophy	Add	54	Total = 46
	Divide '46' by 100 and exponentiate ($e^{0.46}$)		=	1.58

Probability of survival free of stroke, MI or vascular death

At one year $= 0.95^{(1.58)} =$ 0.92 or 92%
At five years $= 0.79^{(1.58)} =$ 0.69 or 69%

Prediction equation for survival free of stroke

	Start			Cumulative score
**	(Age−60)	Multiplied by	4.5	45
	Female	Subtract	36	9
	Amaurosis fugax only	Subtract	72	
	Carotid and vertebrobasilar TIAs	Add	53	
	More than one TIA in last 3 months	Add	$(1.6 \times [n - 1])$	
	Peripheral vascular disease	Add	76	
	Residual neurological signs	Add	68	
**	Left ventricular hypertrophy	Add	74	Total = 77
	Divide '77' by 100 and exponentiate ($e^{0.77}$)		=	2.16

Probability of survival free of stroke

At one year $= 0.965^{(2.16)} =$ 0.92 or 92%
At five years $= 0.88^{(2.16)} =$ 0.76 or 76%

(Table 5 continued)

Prediction equation for survival free of coronary event

		Multiplied by		
**	(Age−60)	Multiplied by	8.1	81
	Female	Subtract	102	−21
	Amaurosis fugax only	Subtract	44	
	Carotid and vertebrobasilar TIAs	Add	107	
	More than one TIA in last 3 months	Add	$(0.97 \times [n - 1])$	
	Peripheral vascular disease	Add	59	
**	Left ventricular hypertrophy	Add	33	12
	Residual neurological signs	Add	48	
	Ischaemic heart disease	Add	87	
	Divide '12' by 100 and exponentiate $(e^{0.12})$		=	Total = 12
				1.13

Probability of survival free of coronary event

At one year = $0.99^{(1.13)}$ =   0.99   or 99%
At five years = $0.92^{(1.13)}$ =   0.91   or 91%

MI = myocardial infarction
TIA = transient ischaemic attack
VB = vertebrobasilar

Table 6. Non-pharmacological therapy for hypertension (see Refs. 13–21).

Diet
—Sodium restriction to 90 mmol/day (2 g sodium or 4 g salt)
—Weight loss to within 15% of ideal body weight
—Alcohol restriction to 1 oz/day (2 oz of 100-proof whisky)
                                (8 oz of wine)
                                (24 oz of beer)
—Fat modification to less saturated fat; more polyunsaturated fat

Regular physical exercise
Psychological techniques
—Biofeedback
—Relaxation

Vascular risk factor reduction
—Smoking
—Cholesterol
—Diabetes
—Obesity

Potassium, calcium, magnesium supplementation (unproven; role not determined)

alcohol.[19–21] If these measures are inappropriate or have been tried without success, pharmacological therapy needs to be considered.

Pharmacological therapy. There is some uncertainty about the level of blood pressure at which drug treatment should begin and whether elderly patients should be treated at all. Treating elderly patients is reasonable, provided that the doctor is aware of potential side-effects, particularly postural hypotension,[22] and that care is taken.

Once a decision has been made to intervene pharmacologically, various drugs can be used. If therapy is chosen carefully, more than half those with mild hypertension can be controlled with a single drug, and more than 90% should be controlled with no more than two.[11] Long-term compliance is an essential element in reducing the morbidity and mortality related to hypertension. Several factors related to the use of specific drugs, including adverse effects, interference with lifestyle, cost and inconvenience of use, play an important role in non-compliance. Thus, drug selection is a critical part of the management of the patient with hypertension.

Which drug? The first choice of pharmacological treatment for hypertension continues to be debated vigorously, but really depends on several of the factors mentioned in the preceding paragraph. Bearing these in mind, most people would still consider diuretics and beta-blockers to be the preferred first choice of treatment for two main reasons:

1. Diuretics and beta-blockers have been shown beyond doubt to reduce the risk of stroke and, less so, of coronary events in hypertensive patients.[10] However, there is no evidence from trials of the effect of the newer classes of drugs (angiotensin-converting enzyme inhibitors (ACEs), calcium antagonists and alpha-blockers) on the incidence of stroke or coronary events. In fact, trials of calcium antagonists after myocardial infarction showed a slight worsening of prognosis.[23] At least ten years is usually required to establish the clinical effects of newer drugs — but some of these 'newer' drugs have been on the market for ten years, and there are still inadequate data.

2. Diuretics and beta-blockers are relatively inexpensive. A one-year's course of bendrofluazide costs £2–4 and beta-blockers, £30–60. For calcium antagonists or ACEs, the cost is £100–200.[24] If between 10% and 20% of the adult population are candidates for lifelong antihypertensive treatment, the issue of cost is obviously important.

Thiazides reduce blood pressure by reducing peripheral resistance rather than by their diuretic effect. Several adverse effects are well recognised:

1. Hypokalaemia: the evidence does not suggest that hypokalaemia induced by thiazides is an important cause of cardiac arrhythmias.

2. Sodium depletion: this is rarely a problem in patients taking thiazide diuretics alone, but may be a problem, particularly in elderly patients, if given together with amiloride (usually as Moduretic).

3. Increased sodium cholesterol concentration, particularly the low density lipoprotein (LDL) fraction. This is only short term; in the long term, the cholesterol concentration falls to baseline concentrations.

4. Worsening of glucose tolerance.

5. Hyperuricaemia occurs in half of all patients, but less than 2% suffer clinical gout.

6. Impotence in men, which is reversible on withdrawal of treatment.

7. Postural hypotension.[25]

8. Concurrent use of non-steroidal anti-inflammatory drugs may blunt the hypotensive effects of thiazides.

Perhaps as a result of either or all the above, the quality of life in patients taking thiazide diuretics may be inferior to that of patients taking beta-blockers. However, the dose commonly used in hypertension has probably been unnecessarily high: cyclopenthiazide, 125 μg, seems as effective as 500 μg.[25]

Beta-blockers also have adverse effects. These include sedation, insomnia, fatigue, cold extremities, exacerbation of symptoms of peripheral vascular disease, chronic obstructive airways disease or asthma, inhibition of many of the warning symptoms of hypoglycaemia, a decrease in high density lipoprotein (HDL) cholesterol, and a negative effect on cardiac conduction and contractility, contraindicating their use in patients with conduction system disease and congestive cardiac failure.

In the 70-year-old patient under discussion, the presence of coexisting atrial fibrillation (particularly if rapid) and mild to moderate hypertension would probably be best treated initially with a small dose of a beta-blocker (eg atenolol 50 mg/day, increasing to 100 mg/day if necessary). If intolerable adverse effects occur, a small dose of the calcium antagonist verapamil (eg 80 mg tds) would be indicated as it dilates arterioles (reducing blood pressure) and delays conduction through the AV node, thus slowing the ventricular rate. Cardiac output is usually unaffected.

Stepped care. Stepped care is a pragmatic and widely used approach to control blood pressure, which involves lowering blood pressure to target levels with low to intermediate doses of one, two or three drugs in combinations that minimise adverse effects. Details of the newer antihypertensive agents are available in extensive reviews.[11,12]

Cigarette smoking

Cigarette smoking is associated with a twofold excess risk of cerebral infarction.[26] The risk is dose-dependent, increasing with the number of cigarettes smoked, and is greater in patients with ischaemic stroke due to extracranial or intracranial vascular disease (relative risk: 5.7; 95% CI: 2.8–12.0) than in patients with ischaemic stroke due to cerebral emboli (relative risk: 0.4; 95% CI: 0.1–1.8).[27]

It has been shown that the mortality hazards of smoking extend well into later life and that by quitting smoking even older smokers with[28] and without[29] existing coronary artery disease can reduce their risk of myocardial infarction and death, even after years of accumulated exposure. Therefore, should the patient described in Chapter 3 stop a 'mere' five cigarettes per day which may be keeping her weight down? Possibly yes, as she has more to gain in terms of reducing her risk of vascular and non-vascular events (eg pulmonary disease), and there is also probably a small financial saving (unless she eats a lot more).

Cholesterol

High plasma cholesterol concentration is strongly associated with increased risk of coronary heart disease,[30] and weakly associated with increased risk of ischaemic stroke.[31,32] If plasma cholesterol concentration is reduced by 10%, mortality from coronary heart disease can be reduced by about 20% over two years.[33] As the attributable risk of coronary heart disease due to hypercholesterolaemia increases with age, cholesterol-lowering interventions should potentially prevent more deaths from coronary heart disease per year among older persons than among middle-aged men.[34,35]

The patient under discussion has a higher risk of a coronary event (about 2% per year) and ischaemic stroke than asymptomatic individuals. It is appropriate therefore to try to reduce this risk by lowering her plasma cholesterol.[36] Dietary regulation is the first approach. The two main dietary factors that influence plasma cholesterol concentration are fat intake and energy balance. The weight of the patient under discussion is not stated. Loss of weight in obese patients is usually attended by a fall both in plasma cholesterol concentration and in serum triglyceride levels and by an increase in HDL cholesterol concentration. A decrease in the intake of saturated fatty acids, provided mainly by dairy fat and fatty meat, is the most important element in a diet to reduce cholesterol. The proportion of energy derived from total fat should be reduced from the average of about 40% to about 30%. Further reduction may lower the concentration of HDL cholesterol and decrease the palatability of the diet. Saturated fats should be limited to less than 10% of the energy intake and replaced by unrefined carbohydrates and monounsaturated or polyunsaturated fatty acids which may lower LDL cholesterol concentration. Enrichment of the diet with monounsaturated fat may not alter the beneficial effects of a low saturated fat diet, but it does permit a greater intake of total calories as fat.[37]

The dietary intake of saturated fatty acids can be reduced considerably by several measures:

- changing to skimmed milk, eating less cheese and using low fat cheese;
- changing from butter or ordinary margarine to a low fat spread or margarine high in polyunsaturated fats;
- changing from hard cooking fats to liquid vegetable oils low in saturated fats (olive, corn, rapeseed, safflower, sunflower, soyabean oils);
- eating more fruit and vegetables; and
- choosing lean cuts of meat and fish.

Grilling rather than frying food can also be helpful. In most people, plasma cholesterol concentration is only mildly influenced by dietary cholesterol, which is provided mainly by eggs. Fish oils have little effect on plasma cholesterol concentration at the doses commonly used, and may even increase LDL in some patients. They are thought to protect against coronary heart disease by mechanisms independent of plasma cholesterol concentration. Advice about dietary change should not be cast in a negative light because this may be mis-interpreted as prohibition of pleasurable and, until now, culturally accepted behaviour.

If dietary manipulation fails to return the lipid levels to normal, consideration of cholesterol-lowering drug therapy is indicated. However, drug treatment is costly and of unknown long-term safety. The decision to use lipid-lowering medication should be based on the premise that the expected benefits will outweigh the risks and costs. The choice of cholesterol-lowering drug will be determined mainly by the dyslipidaemia to be corrected. For most people with moderate hypercholesterolaemia (plasma cholesterol concentrations of 5.2–6.5 mmol/l), dietary advice and correction of other risk factors are appropriate. If plasma concentrations exceed 6.5 mmol/l, more inten-sive dietary intervention and follow-up may be needed, and if greater than 7.5 mmol/l, drug therapy may be indicated, but a recent meta-analysis shows just how limited are the benefits.[38] In this patient, whose cholesterol level is 6.7 mmol/l, dietary advice is the most appropriate management.

Antiplatelet agents

Data from the Antiplatelet Trialists' Collaboration on 29,000 patients with symptomatic vascular disease who were randomised to anti-platelet therapy or no antiplatelet therapy indicated that the former was associated with a 25% reduction in the odds of having a vascular event (stroke, myocardial infarction or vascular death) ($2p < 0.0001$).[39] The reduction in the odds of non-fatal stroke was 27% ($2p < 0.0001$), of non-fatal myocardial infarction, 32% ($2p < 0.0001$), and of vascular death, 15% ($2p = 0.0003$). These results were all highly statistically significant but, more important, the size of the treatment effect was *clinically* significant.

Which agent?

Despite the wealth of data in the overview by the Antiplatelet Trialists' Collaboration,[39,40] there have been few directly randomised comparisons of different antiplatelet regimens. Aspirin has been the most commonly tested agent. It is a simple, cheap and effective treatment, to which the addition of dipyridamole confers no advantage.[40] However, it has not been shown to be any more or less effective than other antiplatelet regimens based on indirect comparisons. Direct comparisons indicate other antiplatelet drugs are no more effective than aspirin, except perhaps ticlopidine, and are more expensive. Ticlopidine is also more toxic than aspirin. The principal adverse effects include diarrhoea and skin rash, but of most concern are the increase in total cholesterol and the infrequent occurrence of neutropenia.[41,42]

Which dose of aspirin?

Aspirin, 300 mg/day, has been shown to be effective. There is no clear evidence that higher doses are more efficacious, whereas the gastric effects (dyspepsia and gastrointestinal bleeding) are directly related to the dose of aspirin.[43,44] Recent trials that have tested doses of aspirin less than 300 mg/day (30 mg/day and 75 mg/day, respectively) have shown that they are as effective as higher doses and are associated with a lower incidence of side-effects.[45,46]

It would seem reasonable to treat initally all suitable patients with aspirin 75–300 mg/day, unless they have a history of previous gastric intolerance. If adverse effects occur, such as dyspepsia and gastrointestinal haemorrhage, which do not resolve with a smaller dose (75 mg or 30 mg daily), the patients should be switched to ticlopidine, if available. Alternatively, sulphinpyrazone, 200 mg qds, may be effective.

What is the risk of intracerebral haemorrhage?

In theory, antiplatelet therapy may increase the risk of intracranial bleeding. Data from the randomised studies on the size of this risk are scanty but compatible with an increased risk of intracerebral haemorrhage of about 1.5,[39,40,43,44,47] but also with a zero excess risk. The absolute increase in number of haemorrhagic strokes is very small and far outweighed by the absolute reduction in the number of ischaemic strokes (Table 7).

Anticoagulation

There have been no randomised trials (except one pilot study) of the risks and benefits of short-term anticoagulation in preventing cerebral infarction in patients with recent TIAs. Occasionally, heparin is given

Table 7. Effect of two years' antiplatelet therapy after a transient ischaemic attack or minor stroke (data from the 1990 meeting of the Antiplatelet Trialists' Collaboration).[40]

Type of stroke	Antiplatelet therapy (%)	Control (%)
Ischaemic stroke	9.7	12.1
Haemorrhagic stroke	0.6	0.4
Total stroke*	10.4	12.8

Net reduction in total stroke 19% (2p <0.00001)

*Note: this includes strokes in which the pathological subtype was not determined.

to patients with crescendo TIAs that have not responded to aspirin, but this is only on an empirical basis.

Only five randomised controlled trials of long-term anticoagulation against no treatment have been undertaken in TIA patients, all far too small ($n = 227$; 26 strokes and 32 deaths) to be able to demonstrate benefit, harm or no effect. Consequently, it is not known whether anticoagulation after TIA is effective, dangerous, both or neither.

The patient being considered had evidence of non-valvular atrial fibrillation which may be a cause of cardiac embolism. Although long-term anticoagulant and/or antiplatelet therapy has been shown to be effective in the primary prevention of stroke or systemic embolism in stroke-free people with atrial fibrillation,[48–52] the value of long-term anticoagulant therapy and platelet anti-aggregant drugs in the secondary prevention of vascular events in patients with TIA or minor ischaemic stroke and non-valvular atrial fibrillation is unproven. However, two large randomised controlled trials are in progress:

- the Veterans Administration (arm II) study comparing oral anticoagulants (INR* 1.5–2.5) and placebo; and

- the European Atrial Fibrillation trial comparing warfarin, aspirin and placebo in patients with non-valvular atrial fibrillation and a TIA or minor ischaemic stroke.

For the patient under discussion, it is impossible to determine the exact cause of the TIA, whether it is artery-to-artery or cardiogenic embolism. In view of the uncertainty about the use of antithrombotic agents in the secondary prevention of cardioembolic events in TIA patients with atrial fibrillation, it would be most appropriate for her to be entered into the European Atrial Fibrillation Trial and randomised

*International Normalised Ratio: a standardised measure of prothrombin ratio.

to either warfarin, aspirin or placebo (for details see end of text). If she does not agree or if she is already to be randomised in another trial, such as the European Carotid Surgery Trial (see below), it would probably be more appropriate to adopt a conservative approach and use aspirin, as opposed to warfarin, as a secondary preventive measure—because aspirin has been shown to be effective, relatively safe, inexpensive and widely available. The dose of aspirin should probably be 300 mg/day because, if atrial fibrillation is important in the pathogenesis of the TIA, this is the lowest dose shown to be effective in atrial fibrillation. If adverse gastrointestinal effects occur, the dose could be lowered sequentially as far as 30 mg/day with effect.

Carotid endarterectomy

In this patient, the presence of an asymptomatic left carotid bruit raises the possibility of left carotid stenosis and the possible benefits (and risks) of performing a carotid endarterectomy to prevent subsequent ischaemic stroke in the left cerebral hemisphere. At present, there is no evidence that this is effective in asymptomatic people, but it may be appropriate for symptomatic carotid ischaemic events.

Carotid endarterectomy has recently been shown to be effective in reducing the risk of stroke in patients with recent non-disabling symptomatic carotid ischaemic events who are fit and willing for surgery and who have severe (70–99%) stenosis of internal carotid artery origin on the symptomatic side.[53,54] The risk of surgery far outweighs the benefits for patients with mild (0–29%) carotid stenosis, but uncertainty remains for those with moderate (30–69%) stenosis, for whom the carotid surgery trials continue (to try to seek the answer). Therefore, several points should be considered:

What does a carotid bruit mean?

A carotid bruit is a clinical sign which usually correlates with underlying carotid stenosis, but it is too inaccurate to rely upon to detect carotid stenosis. Some patients with occlusion of the internal carotid artery have an overlying bruit due to external carotid stenosis, while others with significant stenosis of the internal carotid artery have no bruit (see Fig. 1).[4]

Is an asymptomatic carotid bruit a risk factor for stroke?

Prospective studies on representative samples of persons without previous TIA or stroke who have a carotid bruit suggest that their annual risk of stroke is about 1–2% (95% CI: 0.7–4.6% per year). This is for all forms of stroke (including non-ischaemic stroke), and may not correlate with the vascular territory of the bruit. In fact, most strokes in patients with asymptomatic bruit or stenosis occur in arterial territories unrelated to the carotid artery with the bruit or stenosis. The annual risk of ipsilateral ischaemic thromboembolic stroke may be as low as 0.1%.

Do asymptomatic patients with tight stenosis have a greater risk of stroke than those with lesser stenosis?

There is sufficient evidence now to support such a correlation.[55] However, the risk of serious cardiovascular events also seems to increase with the severity of carotid stenosis and is higher than the risk of stroke.

Can treatment of patients with asymptomatic carotid bruit reduce the risk of stroke?

No randomised controlled trials have tested the efficacy of antiplatelet agents in the primary prevention of stroke for patients with asymptomatic carotid stenosis. Recently, three randomised trials of carotid endarterectomy for asymptomatic carotid stenosis have been published,[56–58] but the results are inconclusive for important outcome events such as stroke and death, so we are awaiting the outcome of the largest trial—the Asymptomatic Carotid Atherosclerosis Study.[59] Clinical practice is currently governed by interpretation of uncontrolled data and these inconclusive trials.

Carotid endarterectomy carries a measurable risk and does not render the patient immune from subsequent stroke. The risk/benefit equation of the procedure must consider the risk of angiography (1%), the skill of the surgeon, the complication rate of the procedure (1–21%), and the annual risk of stroke in the years that follow surgery (1–2% per year). The balance of evidence at present is against angiography and surgery for asymptomatic carotid bruit.

Does the patient have tight extracranial internal carotid stenosis on the symptomatic side?

This patient has suffered a non-disabling carotid ischaemic event, and is at risk to suffer another such event which may be disabling or even fatal. It is possible that a carotid endarterectomy would significantly reduce her chance of an ipsilateral ischaemic stroke, provided that she has 70–99% stenosis of the origin of the internal carotid artery on the symptomatic side (or possibly 30–69% stenosis, depending on the results of the on-going carotid surgery trials), *and* that the combined radiological and surgical morbidity and mortality rates of the surgeon and neuroradiologist in the particular medical institution are similar to those recorded in the carotid surgery trials (ie < 10%). Although she does not have a bruit over the carotid artery on the symptomatic side, this does not mean that she does not have tight stenosis that may be operable.[4]

The first question to ask the patient is whether she would consider undergoing carotid endarterectomy if a tight stenosis can be demonstrated. If the answer is in the affirmative, the most cost-effective strategy is first to image the extracranial carotid arteries non-invasively (and therefore safely) by duplex ultrasound.[4] For detecting carotid stenosis of more than 50%, the sensitivity of duplex is about 94–100% and the specificity about 84–96%.[60]

The patient would be considered for entry into the European Carotid Surgery Trial with 30–69% stenosis of the symptomatic carotid, or for carotid surgery with 70–99% stenosis, so the aim of the duplex is to see whether there is more than about 30% stenosis of the origin of the internal carotid artery on the symptomatic side. If there is 70–99% stenosis, carotid angiography is indicated because most surgeons are unwilling to consider surgery on the basis of carotid ultrasound studies alone. The risk of a permanent disabling stroke following carotid angiography is about 1%.[61] If the angiogram shows 70–99% stenosis, and if the patient is willing and medically fit for surgery (ie does not have uncontrolled hypertension or angina), a surgical consultation is appropriate. If 30–69% stenosis is demonstrated, the patient should be counselled on the potential risks and benefits of carotid surgery, and offered entry and randomisation in the European Carotid Surgery Trial.

Addresses for entering patients into trials

European Atrial Fibrillation Trial

Dr Anet van Latum
EAFT
Institute of Neurology Ee2287
Erasmus University Rotterdam
PO Box 1738
3000 DR Rotterdam
The Netherlands

European Carotid Surgery Trial

Professor CP Warlow
Department of Clinical Neurosciences
Western General Hospital
Edinburgh EH4 2XU
UK

References

1. Dennis MS, Bamford JM, Sandercock PAG, Warlow CP. Incidence of transient ischaemic attacks in Oxfordshire, England. *Stroke* 1989; **20**: 333–9
2. Kraaijeveld CL, van Gijn J, Schouten HJA, Staal A. Interobserver agreement for the diagnosis of transient ischaemic attacks. *Stroke* 1984; **15**: 723–5
3. Hankey GJ, Warlow CP. Lacunar transient ischaemic attacks: a clinically useful concept? *Lancet* 1991; **337**: 335–8
4. Hankey GJ, Warlow CP. Symptomatic carotid ischaemic events: safest and most cost effective way of selecting patients for angiography, before carotid endarterectomy. *British Medical Journal* 1990; **300**: 1485–1591
5. Chesebro JH, Fuster V, Halperin JL. Atrial fibrillation-risk marker for stroke. *New England Journal of Medicine* 1990; **323**: 1556–8
6. Hankey GJ, Slattery JM, Warlow CP. The prognosis of hospital-referred transient ischaemic attacks. *Journal of Neurology, Neurosurgery and Psychiatry* 1991; **54**: 793–802
7. Dennis M, Bamford J, Sandercock P, Warlow C. Prognosis of transient ischaemic attacks in the Oxfordshire Community Stroke Project. *Stroke* 1990; **21**: 848–53
8. Hankey GJ, Slattery JM, Warlow CP. Transient ischaemic attacks. Which patients are at high (and low) risk of serious vascular events? *Journal of Neurology, Neurosurgery and Psychiatry* 1992; **55**: 640–52
9. MacMahon S, Peto R, Cutler J, *et al*. Blood pressure, stroke and coronary heart disease. Part 1. Prolonged differences in blood pressure: prospective observational studies corrected for the regression dilution bias. *Lancet* 1990; **335**: 765–74
10. Collins R, Peto R, MacMahon S, *et al*. Blood pressure, stroke and coronary heart disease. Part 2. Short-term reductions in blood pressure: overview of randomised drug trials in their epidemiological context. *Lancet* 1990; **335**: 827–38
11. Schwartz GL. Initial therapy for hypertension-individualising care. *Mayo Clinic Proceedings* 1990; **65**: 73–87
12. Jennings GL, Sudhir K. Initial therapy of primary hypertension. *Medical Journal of Australia* 1990; **152**: 198–203
13. Law MR, Frost CD, Wald NJ. By how much does dietary salt reduction lower blood pressure? I—Analysis of observational data among populations. *British Medical Journal* 1991; **302**: 811–5

14. Frost CD, Law MR, Wald NJ. By how much does dietary salt reduction lower blood pressure? III—Analysis of data from trials of salt reduction. *British Medical Journal* 1991; **302**: 819–24

15. Law MR, Frost CD, Wald NJ. By how much does dietary salt reduction lower blood pressure? II—Analysis of observational data within populations. *British Medical Journal* 1991; **302**: 815–8

16. Tobian L. Hypertension and obesity. *New England Journal of Medicine* 1978; **298**: 46–7

17. Reisin E, Frohlich ED, Messerli FH, *et al.* Cardiovascular change after weight reduction in obesity hypertension. *Annals of Internal Medicine* 1983; **98**: 315–9

18. Beilin LJ. Diet and hypertension: critical concepts and controversies. *Journal of Hypertension* 1987; **5** (suppl 5): S447–57

19. Arkwright PD, Beilin LJ, Rouse I, *et al.* Effects of alcohol use and other aspects of life-style on blood pressure levels and prevalence of hypertension in a working population. *Circulation* 1982; **66**: 60–6

20. Puddey IB, Beilin LJ, Vandongen R, *et al.* Evidence for a direct effect of alcohol consumption on blood pressure in normotensive man—a randomised controlled trial. *Hypertension* 1985; **7**: 707–13

21. Puddey IB, Beilin LJ, Vandongen R. Regular alcohol use raises blood pressure in treated hypertensive subjects—a randomised controlled trial. *Lancet* 1987; **i**: 647–51

22. Hankey GJ, Gubbay SS. Focal cerebral ischaemia and infarction due to antihypertensive therapy. *Medical Journal of Australia* 1987; **146**: 412–4

23. Yusuf S. The use of beta-adrenergic agents, iv nitrates and calcium channel blocking agents following acute myocardial infarction. *Chest* 1988; **93**: 25–8S

24. Swales JD. First line treatment in hypertension. *British Medical Journal* 1990; **301**: 1172–3

25. Orme M. Thiazides in the 1990s. *British Medical Journal* 1990; **300**: 1668–9

26. Shinton R, Beevers G. Meta-analysis of relation between cigarette smoking and stroke. *British Medical Journal* 1989; **298**: 789–94

27. Donnan GA, McNeil JJ, Adena MA, Doyle AE, O'Malley HMO, Neill GC. Smoking as a risk factor for cerebral ischaemia. *Lancet* 1989; **ii**: 643–7

28. Hermanson B, Omenn GS, Kronmal RA, Gersh BJ. Participants in the Coronary Artery Surgery Study: beneficial six-year outcome of smoking cessation in older men and women with coronary artery disease: results from the CASS registry. *New England Journal of Medicine* 1988; **319**: 1365–9

29. LaCroix AZ, Lang J, Scherr P, *et al.* Smoking and mortality among older men and women in three communities. *New England Journal of Medicine* 1991; **324**: 1619–25

30. Rose G, Shipley M. Plasma cholesterol concentration and death from coronary heart disease: 10 year results of the Whitehall study. *British Medical Journal* 1986; **293**: 306–7

31. Iso H, Jacobs DR, Wentworth D, Neaton JD, Cohen JD (for the MRFIT Research Group). Serum cholesterol levels and six-year mortality from stroke in 350,977 men screened for the multiple risk factor intervention trial. *New England Journal of Medicine* 1989; **320**: 904–10

32. Qizilbash N, Jones L, Warlow C, Mann J. Fibrinogen and lipid concentrations as risk factors for transient ischaemic attacks and minor ischaemic strokes. *British Medical Journal* 1991; **303**: 605–9

33. Peto R, Yusuf S, Collins R. Cholesterol lowering trial results in their epidemiological context. *Circulation* 1985; **72** (suppl III): 451 (abstract)

34. Gordon DJ, Rifkind BM. Treating high blood pressure cholesterol in the older patient. *American Journal of Cardiology* 1989; **63**: 48H–52H

35. Rubin SM, Sidney S, Black DM, Browner WS, Hulley SB, Cummings SR. High blood cholesterol in elderly men and the excess risk for coronary heart disease. *Annals of Internal Medicine* 1990; **113**: 916–20

36. Kafonek SD, Kwiterovich PO. Treatment of hypercholesterolemia in the elderly. *Annals of Internal Medicine* 1990; **112**: 723–5

37. Ginsberg HN, Barr SL, Gilbert A, *et al.* Reduction of plasma cholesterol levels in normal men on an American Heart Association Step I Diet or a Step I Diet with added monounsaturated fat. *New England Journal of Medicine* 1990; **322**: 574–9

38. Davey Smith G, Song F, Sheldon TA. Cholesterol lowering and mortality: the importance of considering initial level of risk. *British Medical Journal* 1993; **306**: 1367–73

39. Antiplatelet Trialists' Collaboration. Secondary prevention of vascular disease by prolonged antiplatelet treatment. *British Medical Journal* 1988; **296**: 320–31

40. Antiplatelet Trialists' Collaboration. Collaborative overview of randomised trials of antiplatelet treatment. Part 1. Prevention of death, myocardial infarction and stroke by prolonged antiplatelet therapy in various categories of patients. *British Medical Journal* 1993 (in press)

41. Hass WK, Easton JD, Adams HP, *et al.* Ticlopidine Aspirin Stroke Study Group: a randomised trial comparing ticlopidine hydrochloride with aspirin for the prevention of stroke in high-risk patients. *New England Journal of Medicine* 1989; **321**: 501–7

42. Warlow CP. Ticlopidine, a new antithrombotic drug: but is it better than aspirin for long term use? *Journal of Neurology, Neurosurgery and Psychiatry* 1990; **53**: 185–7

43. UK-TIA Study Group. United Kingdom transient ischaemic attack (UK-TIA) aspirin trial: interim results. *British Medical Journal* 1988; **296**: 316–20

44. UK-TIA Study Group. United Kingdom transient ischaemic attack (UK-TIA) aspirin trial: final results. *Journal of Neurology, Neurosurgery and Psychiatry* 1991; **54**: 1044–54

45. The Dutch TIA Trial Study Group. A comparison of two doses of aspirin (30 mg vs. 283 mg a day) in patients after a transient ischemic attack or minor ischemic stroke. *New England Journal of Medicine* 1991; **325**: 1261–6

46. The SALT Collaborative Group. Swedish Aspirin Low-dose Trial (SALT) of 75 mg aspirin as secondary prophylaxis after cerebrovascular ischaemic events. *Lancet* 1991; **338**: 1345–9

47. Hennekens CH, Buring JE, Sandercock P, Collins R, Peto R. Aspirin and other antiplatelet agents in the secondary and primary prevention of cardiovascular disease. *Circulation* 1989; **80**: 749–56

48. Petersen P, Boysen G, Godtfredsen J, Andersen E, Andersen B. Placebo-

controlled randomised trial of warfarin and aspirin for prevention of thromboembolic complications in chronic atrial fibrillation: the Copenhagen AFASAK study. *Lancet* 1989; **i**: 175–9

49. Stroke Prevention in Atrial Fibrillation Investigators. Stroke Prevention in Atrial Fibrillation Study: final results. *Circulation* 1991; **84**: 527–39

50. The Boston Area Anticoagulation Trial for Atrial Fibrillation Investigators. The effect of low-dose warfarin on the risk of stroke in patients with nonrheumatic atrial fibrillation. *New England Journal of Medicine* 1990; **323**: 1505–11

51. Connolly SJ, Laupacis A, Gent M, Roberts RS, Cairns JA, Joyner C. Canadian Atrial Fibrillation Anticoagulation (CAFA) Study. *Journal of the American College of Cardiology* 1991; **18**: 349–55

52. Ezekowitz MD, Bridgers SL, James KE, *et al.* Warfarin in the prevention of stroke associated with nonrheumatic atrial fibrillation. *New England Journal of Medicine* 1992; **327**: 1406–12

53. European Carotid Surgery Trialists' Collaborative Group. MRC European Carotid Surgery Trial: interim results for symptomatic patients with severe (70–99%) or with mild (0–29%) carotid stenosis. *Lancet* 1991; **337**: 1235–43

54. North American Symptomatic Carotid Endarterectomy Trial Collaborators, 1991. Beneficial effect of carotid endarterectomy in symptomatic patients with high-grade carotid stenosis. *New England Journal of Medicine* 1991; **325**: 445–53

55. Chambers BR, Norris JW. Outcome in patients with asymptomatic neck bruits. *New England Journal of Medicine* 1986; **315**: 860–5

56. The CASANOVA Study Group. Carotid surgery versus medical therapy in asymptomatic carotid stenosis. *Stroke* 1991; **22**: 1229–35

57. Mayo Asymptomatic Carotid Endarterectomy Study Group. Results of a randomized controlled trial of carotid endarterectomy for asymptomatic carotid stenosis. *Mayo Clinic Proceedings* 1992; **67**: 513–8

58. Hobson RW II, Weiss DG, Fields WS, *et al.* Efficacy of carotid endarterectomy for asymptomatic carotid stenosis. *New England Journal of Medicine* 1993; **328**: 221–7

59. The Asymptomatic Carotid Atherosclerosis Study Group. Study design for randomized prospective trial of carotid endarterectomy for asymptomatic atherosclerosis. *Stroke* 1989; **20**: 844–9

60. Lewis BD, James M, Welch TJ. Current applications of duplex and colour flow doppler ultrasound imaging: carotid and peripheral vascular system. *Mayo Clinic Proceedings* 1989; **64**: 1147–57

61. Hankey GJ, Warlow CP, Sellar RJ. Cerebral angiographic risk in mild cerebrovascular disease. *Stroke* 1990; **21**: 209–22

7 | Clinical decision analysis: an application to the management of an elderly person with hypertension who has had a transient ischaemic attack

Jack Dowie*, Graeme Hankey[†] and Huw Llewelyn[‡]

The case of an elderly female patient presenting with features suggestive of a transient ischaemic attack (TIA) was discussed in Chapter 6. The clinicians responsible reported their judgements and decisions and explained the reasoning behind them.

In this chapter we report the results of a 'second opinion', based not on clinical judgement but on a modest 'clinical decision analysis' of this case. The use of the qualifier 'modest' is intended to give an accurate representation of the quality of this particular effort in relation to what might have been attempted with greater time and resources. However, it should not be inferred that this is not regarded as a serious analysis, nor that its insights and conclusions are unworthy of consideration alongside those arrived at by clinical reasoning.

It is important to recognise that documenting the complexities and uncertainties of the case, as was done in exemplary fashion by the clinicians in the previous chapter, cannot establish that a simplified decision analytic modelling of it is not capable of producing a good, or even better, management decision. Clinicians exercising their clinical judgement obviously intend to take into account the complexities and uncertainties of cases they face, but the issue is not one of intention, but of accomplishment. How successful are they in processing all the complexities and uncertainties they have identified in a case, and how well are these integrated into the management decision?

The appropriate comparator for the modest decision analysis reported below is not therefore some notionally 'perfect' decision analysis of the case — by which standard it would fail – but the alternative mode of

*Faculty of Social Sciences, The Open University, Milton Keynes, †Department of Clinical Neurosciences, Western General Hospital, Edinburgh, and ‡School of Medicine and Dentistry, King's College, London.

decision making which is on offer. We believe that the rudimentary analysis carried out here provides significant insight into the case, confirming the conventional analysis in many respects but suggesting that it is lacking in one major respect.

Most important of all, as with any decision analysis, the structure, assumptions and data used in arriving at this 'second opinion' are available for all to see, criticise and vary.

Structuring the case

There are assumed to be three broad management options:

1. Lifestyle advice about smoking and diet. (One simplification in our analysis involves making the fairly realistic assumption that the patient will not comply with such advice.)
2. Medication, of which there are seven possibilities (aspirin, anti-hypertensive drugs and warfarin, individually and in all possible combinations).
3. Surgical management, beginning with Doppler ultrasound, and proceeding to carotid surgery if the scan is suggestive of severe stenosis and if this is confirmed by arteriography. We assume that this route is taken only if there is a firm commitment by both patient and physician to angiography when stenosis is severe on ultrasound, and to surgery if this is confirmed by angiography. If stenosis is of moderate or low degree on ultrasound, or if a tight stenosis on ultrasound is not confirmed on angiography, it is assumed that the patient will be treated medically using the best medical option identified in our analysis.

The option of entering the patient into a clinical trial was not considered for reasons which will be explained following the presentation of the results.

Whichever of these nine management options is adopted, we identify four possible subsequent events (except in the case where surgical death occurs):

1. No untoward event
2. Cerebral infarct
3. Cerebral haemorrhage
4. Systemic haemorrhage

Each of the three adverse events (2–4) is in turn seen as leading to three possible final outcome states:

1. Alive and with no long-term disability
2. Alive but disabled
3. Dead

However, while these are the only 'final' outcomes, the actual final outcome state in any individual scenario incorporates an adjustment for the 'intermediate' effects involved in the particular scenario, eg the side-effects of medication, the experience of undergoing surgery and its precursors, or simply the negative effects of an adverse event.

The 103 resulting scenarios for this patient are set out on the decision tree in Fig. 1 with continuations in Figs. 2 and 3.

In Fig. 1 the tree starts with the nine 'option branches' growing out from the 'decision node' (conventionally represented by a square box). Uncertainties about the future course of events are then represented (in Fig. 2) by the grafting, at each of the round 'chance nodes', of 'chance branches' that represent each of the possible resolutions of the uncertainty concerned. The 'subtree' in Fig. 2 grows out of the lifestyle branch and of each medication option branch, and is also entered when

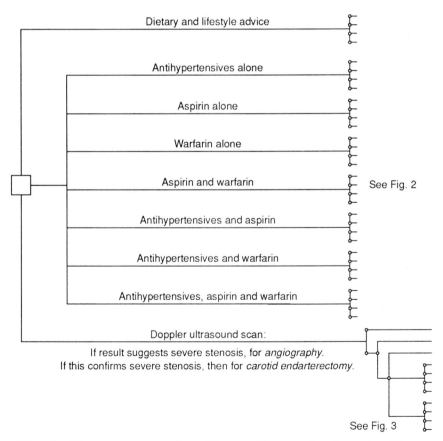

Dietary and lifestyle advice

Antihypertensives alone

Aspirin alone

Warfarin alone

Aspirin and warfarin   See Fig. 2

Antihypertensives and aspirin

Antihypertensives and warfarin

Antihypertensives, aspirin and warfarin

Doppler ultrasound scan:
If result suggests severe stenosis, for *angiography.*
If this confirms severe stenosis, then for *carotid endarterectomy.*

See Fig. 3

Fig. 1. *The management options. The possible scenarios for each option are symbolised by the small subtrees at the end of each option branch. These are presented in detail in Figs. 2 and 3.*

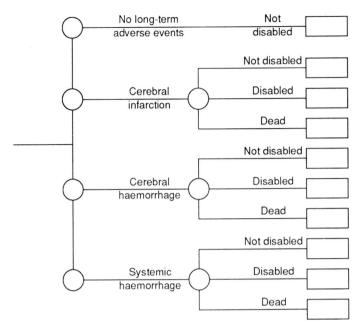

Fig. 2. *The possible scenarios for non-surgical management options. There are ten possible outcomes: three possible outcomes for each of the three possible adverse events, plus 'no adverse event'.*

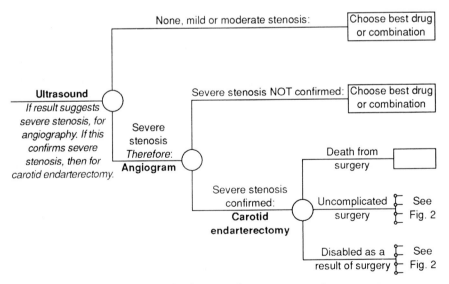

Fig. 3. *The possible scenarios for the surgical management option.*

surgical management is abandoned in favour of medication. One set of chance nodes on this subtree relates to the uncertainty surrounding the occurrence of adverse events, the possibilities being: none, cerebral infarct, cerebral haemorrhage and systemic haemorrhage. The second set relates to the final outcome states that may result from any of these events, the possibilities being: no disability, disability or death. These constitute the 'outcome nodes' of the subtree (conventionally represented by a rectangle).

Fig. 3 presents the somewhat more complicated subtree for the surgical management option, incorporating chance nodes for the results of the scan (and, where undertaken, the angiogram) and for carotid endarterectomy (and subsequent events) if this is performed.

The time horizon for the analysis is five years, and it is assumed that any untoward event (and any resulting death or disability) occurs at the same time whichever branch is followed. Arbitrarily this is taken to be halfway through the period.

Assessment of probabilities and utilities

For each possibility arising at every chance node a probability is needed. Where available, these were obtained from the scientific literature (see Chapter 6), but in many cases the medical literature did not contain anything relevant to the needed figure and in these cases the clinical author was asked to produce his best subjective assessments. To simplify the analysis he was asked to produce assessments conditional on all the evidence considered so far on a branch.

These 'baseline' probabilities may be changed to reflect local conditions or patients, and the impact of the change on the decision identified. The striking feature of the present probability estimates is their similarity across the options. This makes it likely that utility variations will dominate the conclusion of the analysis. In this respect, the present case closely parallels the prostatectomy study of Barry *et al.*[1]

The 'baseline' utilities used in the analysis are purely subjective assessments by the analysts. Research into patient utilities — average or individual — is in its infancy (see Chapter 9). It is, of course, the individual patient's utilities that should be incorporated into a clinical decision analysis.

The utility range is (arbitrarily, but conventionally) set at 0 to 1.0. Surgical death is assigned 0, and 1.0 is taken to represent survival for five years (or more) with no adverse events and no lifestyle change. Death halfway through the five-year period is placed at 0.3, to incorporate a time discount effect.

In decision analysis the patient is not asked directly whether or not he or she will accept surgery or any other intervention as a procedure, instead being asked to provide a value for a final outcome state that incorporates the experience of surgery or other intervention. Negative adjustments of the size reported in Table 1 were therefore made in respect of:

  (i) the adverse events that may occur to a patient (excluding those who die under surgery);

 (ii) the implications and side-effects of medications; and

(iii) the disutilities of the various aspects of surgical management.

Table 1. Adjustments (all negative) to utilities of outcomes for a patient who has had a transient ischaemic attack.

	Negative utility
The various adverse events were assigned the following negative utility:	
Non-disabling cerebral infarct	0.05
Disabling cerebral infarct	0.25
Non-disabling cerebral haemorrhage	0.15
Disabling cerebral haemorrhage	0.45
Non-disabling systemic haemorrhage	0.15
Disabling systemic haemorrhage	0.55
The various drug treatments and their side-effects were assigned the following negative utility (for the whole period of treatment):	
Aspirin	0.01
Antihypertensives	0.02
Warfarin	0.03
Aspirin and antihypertensives	0.03
Aspirin and warfarin	0.04
Antihypertensives and warfarin	0.05
Aspirin, antihypertensives and warfarin	0.06
The procedures involved in the surgical option were assigned the following negative utility:	
Ultrasound	0.01
Angiography	0.02
Ultrasound and angiography	$0.01 + 0.02 = 0.03$
Carotid endarterectomy	0.03
Ultrasound, angiography and carotid endarterectomy	$0.01 + 0.02 + 0.03 = 0.06$

To illustrate: if a patient on 'antihypertensives only' suffers a disabling cerebral infarction during the five-year period but does not die, the outcome utility is 1.0 minus 0.25 for the cerebral infarction-induced disability, minus another 0.02 for the disutility of antihypertensive medication, or 0.73.

This utility will be found in the appropriate place on the subtree for the option 'antihypertensive medication only' that appears as Fig. 4.

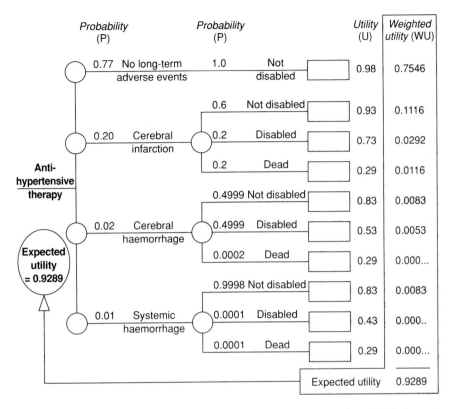

Fig. 4. *The subtree for the 'antihypertensives only' option, with probabilities and utilities entered and showing how expected utility for the option is arrived at.*

Calculating the optimal strategy

For each option the 'expected utility' is calculated, where 'expected' is being used in its mathematical sense of 'average'. The utility of each of the possible final outcomes that may result from following the option is weighted by its probability of occurrence.

Referring again to the 'antihypertensive only' subtree in Fig. 4, the outcome just discussed (with a utility of 0.73) has a 0.04 chance of occurring – there is a 0.2 chance of a cerebral infarct and a 0.2 chance of this cerebral infarct resulting in disability. Multiplying the utility of 0.73 by the probability of 0.04 produces the 'weighted utility' of 0.0292 shown in the panel to the right of the tree. Equivalent figures are arrived at for each of the other outcomes for this option, and these are all added together to produce the expected utility for the option. (Note that the 'weighted utilities' for each scenario are *not* expected utilities and have no meaning except as part of the expected utility calculation for the option.)

On our baseline assessments 'antihypertensives only' emerges as the optimal management strategy.*

Table 2 presents the expected utility for each of the nine options, their rank order and the difference between the expected utility for the option concerned and that for 'antihypertensives only' (that with the highest expected utility in the baseline analysis). A summary decision tree is shown in Fig. 5.

Table 2. Baseline results.

Treatment option	Expected utility	Rank order	Difference from first ranked
Lifestyle advice	0.915	4	0.014
Antihypertensives	0.929	1	
Aspirin	0.922	2	0.007
Warfarin	0.894	7	0.035
Aspirin and warfarin	0.877	9	0.052
Aspirin and antihypertensives	0.917	3	0.012
Antihypertensives and warfarin	0.902	6	0.027
Aspirin, antihypertensives and warfarin	0.881	8	0.048
Surgical management	0.913	5	0.016

The expected utility figures (eg the 0.929 for 'antihypertensives only') have no meaning in themselves, nor does the difference between any single pair of expected utilities (eg the difference of 0.007 between antihypertensives and aspirin) have a meaningful interpretation. Utilities, like temperatures, are measured on an *interval* scale, so only differences between pairs of expected utilities can validly be compared. The only type of statement that can legitimately be made on the basis of Table 2 is of the following kind: the loss resulting from setting out on the surgical route as against adopting the 'antihypertensive only' option is roughly twice as great as the loss from adopting the 'aspirin only' option as against the 'antihypertensive only' one; in other words, 0.016 is roughly twice as great as 0.007.

The presentation of results to three or four decimal places should not be regarded as embodying 'spurious precision'. We have chosen to present the precise results of the raw calculations simply so that the calculations are reproducible by others who may wish to explore the tree.

Any error or bias in the baseline assessments used in the analysis will of course be reflected in these expected utility calculations. The

*The subtrees for the options other than 'antihypertensives only', showing how the expected utility of each was reached, are reproduced in Appendix 1 on pages 157–62.

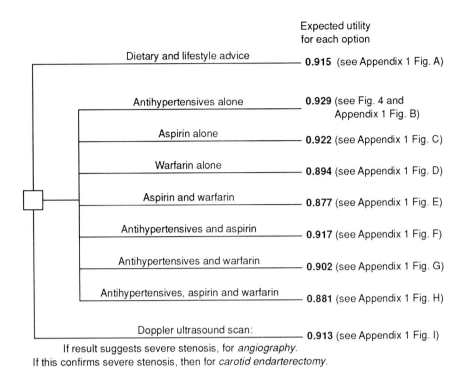

Expected utility
for each option

Dietary and lifestyle advice ——————— 0.915 (see Appendix 1 Fig. A)

Antihypertensives alone   0.929 (see Fig. 4 and
                                          Appendix 1 Fig. B)

Aspirin alone ——————— 0.922 (see Appendix 1 Fig. C)

Warfarin alone ——————— 0.894 (see Appendix 1 Fig. D)

Aspirin and warfarin ——————— 0.877 (see Appendix 1 Fig. E)

Antihypertensives and aspirin ——————— 0.917 (see Appendix 1 Fig. F)

Antihypertensives and warfarin ——————— 0.902 (see Appendix 1 Fig. G)

Antihypertensives, aspirin and warfarin ——————— 0.881 (see Appendix 1 Fig. H)

Doppler ultrasound scan: ——————— 0.913 (see Appendix 1 Fig. I)
If result suggests severe stenosis, for *angiography*.
If this confirms severe stenosis, then for *carotid endarterectomy*.

Fig. 5. *Summary tree showing expected utility of each management option.*

variances of so few of the assessments are known that no attempt has been made to estimate confidence intervals. Are the rankings and differences in Table 2 highly sensitive to trivial changes in the data?

The appropriate response to this question in decision analysis is to undertake a sensitivity analysis. This involves recalculating the tree to see what happens if the numbers are varied over credible ranges.

As an example of sensitivity analysis from the probability side, it may be noted that the baseline conclusion is not affected by any reduction in the surgical complication rate. This was estimated to be 6%, but even if it were zero (still assuming a 1% surgical mortality) surgical management does not emerge as optimal.

On the other hand, and turning to the utility side, a negative allowance of 0.06 was assigned to the inconvenience, discomfort and other disutility of the investigations and procedures associated with surgery. If no negative allowance had been made, recalculation of the tree shows surgical management emerging as the best option (other things unchanged). The 'threshold value' for the disutility of surgery and its investigative precursors — the value which 'flips' the decision in favour of surgical management — is therefore in the 0 to 0.06 range on our particular utility scale.

Further sensitivity analysis confirms that the management decision which is the focus of this analysis is highly sensitive to small variations in several of the utility adjustments in addition to those for surgery, underlining the importance of the patient's own valuation. More serious analysis would therefore require systematic empirical work on the utility side, and in view of this further sensitivity explorations on the probability side were not pursued.

Two points need to be cleared up before concluding. First, why was entry into a clinical trial not considered as an option? By definition, trial enrolment cannot be the optimal strategy for a patient, unless the two arms of the trial have equal expected utility for him or her after a decision analysis of the above sort. The expected value of two expected utilities cannot be greater than the higher one. Whether such equality exists is something to be determined by the decision analysis, in the light of the utilities for the individual patient. (We have also assumed that patients do not gain any utility from trial participation *per se*. They may well do so, but again this is something to be determined with the individual patient.)

Secondly, it will be evident that the analysis has been carried out without any attention to the resource implications of the various options. While such costs can be incorporated into decision analysis, we have taken the view that this illustrative application should not confuse the issue of decision analysis with that of resource allocation, even at the level of the individual clinician.

Conclusion

The most important point to emphasise is that the conclusion of any clinical decision analysis is dependent on the model generated and on the quantitative assessments fed into it. Given our tree structure and probability assessments, antihypertensive medication emerges as the best option for a patient of the type described whose utilities match those which have been entered in our baseline analysis. But, since other patients may well have different utilities from her (and from each other) there can be no universally optimal option, even for those who are medically identical to this patient.

The importance of eliciting carefully and systematically a patient's utilities, especially for those states which involve surgery, is dramatically confirmed in this limited analysis. Such elicitation needs to be done in the context of a careful and systematic exploration of patients' views on all possible outcome states, otherwise the essential comparative dimension of utility analysis — and indeed decision analysis — will be lost, along with most of the potential benefits of undertaking it.

Reference

1. Barry MJ, Mulley AG, Fowler FJ, Wennberg, JW. Watchful waiting vs immediate transurethral resection for symptomatic prostatism: the importance of patients' preferences. *Journal of the American Medical Association* 1988; **259**: 3010–7

8 | Practical steps in setting up a decision support system

Peter Emerson* and Charles Pantin[†]

Decision aids have been implemented in industry much more widely than in medicine.[1] The basic reasons are that, in industry, both the problems and the data are well-defined, partly because they solve problems on systems and mechanisms created by man and because the knowledge is based on measurement of length, breadth, radius, depth of drilling etc. Medicine often relies on data collected from patients or elicited by clinical staff, such as symptoms and signs. In the neurological example outlined in Chapter 3, hard measurement is provided by the appearance of a computerised tomographic scan or the degree of stenosis demonstrated on carotid angiography. However, the symptoms and signs to make a diagnosis of transient ischaemic attack (TIA) are often missing, and the interobserver variation in the diagnosis is high. Hard measurements are usually quicker and easier to collect in industry, so time for development of the decision aid is shorter in industry than in medicine.

Another reason for the greater acceptance of decision aids in industry is that the evaluation of the system is relatively easy. If it works, the parts will fit and/or be fitted quicker. Success or failure is likely to be measured in terms of money saved or lost. Any aid for decision making in clinical medicine should be evaluated with the rigour of a clinical trial if it is to be accepted into practice.[2] This costs time and money.

In this chapter it is suggested how a decision aid might be built to address one or more of the neurological problems described in Chapter 3. Similar ideas, but in the context of the development of a decision aid for chest pain, are explored more fully by Wyatt and Emerson.[3]

Definition of the domain of the decision aid

Several decision aids could be built to help the management of a patient with a transient focal neurological dysfunction of sudden onset. The

Coding and Clinical Information System Development Project, London and †Department of Respiratory Physiology, City General Hospital, Stoke-on-Trent.

111

first would establish the diagnosis, and others might advise on treatment of the conditions found. Thus, the problem which the decision aid addresses must be defined:

- Is it diagnosis or treatment?
- Is there a perceived need for such an aid?
- Can the advice be made available to the users at the right place and time?

A protocol must be written to define the domain of the decision aid and how it is to be evaluated:

- What is the definition of a patient with TIA?
- How will the data be collected?
- What is the 'correct' answer to the problem?
- Is there a clear-cut outcome of an intervention or of not intervening, eg death from stroke or myocardial infarction?
- Will the decision aid be evaluated against the decisions of a panel of experts?
- Is the study ethical?

Definition of first-phase indicants

It is necessary to select those items of data, the indicants, the presence or absence of which may affect the diagnosis or decision under consideration. Indicants may be items of past history, symptoms, signs or results of investigations. There may be different opinions about their importance, so the initial list may be long (up to 50 items[4]). The choice of indicants, for example in the decision analysis for treatment of TIA, will be strongly influenced by the knowledge already gained from clinical trials and other research (see Chapter 6).

The first prospective study

The first set of indicants can now be collected from a series of patients meeting the defined constraints of the domain and in which the 'correct' answer for each case can be found. Problems may arise with the time-scale of the outcome. In the diagnosis of TIA, a panel of experts could be used to give the 'correct' answer reasonably quickly. However, in a decision analysis for treatment of TIA, the outcome (eg a stroke or death) may have to be collected over years (see Tables 4 and 5, Chapter 6).

When the indicants and the 'correct' answer are known, the likelihood ratios can be calculated as described in Chapters 4 and 5. A likelihood ratio of 1 means that the indicant is equally likely to be present in patients with or without the disease or defined characteristic. It is, therefore, a useless predictor, whereas indicants with likelihood ratios of 3 or more are likely to be good predictors.

In this first study, interobserver error should be calculated with at least two clinicians independently interviewing each patient and reviewing each investigation.

The prototype decision aid

Designing and building

The initial study will guide the choice of an appropriate reasoning technique. Close collaboration with the targeted users of the aid will help specify not only the user interface but also the logic of the system.

Examples of non-interactive interfaces include a paper-based algorithm or simple scoring system displayed as written guidelines or on a computer screen as a service provided by a hospital information system. Interactive interfaces include a computer system into which the end-user inputs data by the use of a keyboard, mouse, or some other input device such as a touch screen.

The prototype is then built with the selected reasoning technique and user interface. The probability-based approach (see Chapters 2 and 4) is helpful as the initial technique. The discipline of thinking in probabilistic terms, and in having the predictive probabilities expressed as numbers, may provide a valuable insight into the suitability of the indicants and/or combinations of indicants, even if the Bayesian approach is later modified or even abandoned in favour of a rule-based system.

Testing and modification

The prototype will be tested on the original learning set of patients but, as these were the cases on which the likelihood ratios were calculated, the results may be overly encouraging.

The next step is to test the system prospectively on a new set of patients and reassess the predictive performance. The results are likely to be less encouraging this time. However, more data will now have been collected and the likelihood ratios can be recalculated and modified. This iterative process of testing and modification will continue until further recalculation of the likelihood ratios no longer changes the predictive performance. By this time, a learning data-base of several hundred patients should have been collected. (A large number of patients will be required as the data-base should include at least five cases of each diagnosis or decision, per indicant used.[5]) During this time, the original reasoning technique may have been modified or totally changed because any errors will have been scrutinised to see why some predictions were wrong. Sometimes, 'safety net' clinical rules are required to override a high calculated probability: for example, an affirmative answer to the question, 'does general clinical examination suggest that the patient is too ill to have a carotid angiogram?'

Further trials

When the system has stabilised on the learning data-base, a prospective evaluation of a new test set of data should be undertaken.[2] Testing is easier if a correct answer to the clinical problem addressed is available (ie a gold standard of some kind). Error rates or receiver-operating characteristic curves can be calculated to show how the system performs. If there is no correct answer but only the opinions of experts, the system's performance should be assessed by peer review. In this case, a different panel of experts from the panel constituted for early prospective studies should provide the 'correct' answers against which the system is assessed.

Further questions that both users and experts should address are:

- Is the system pleasant and easy to use?
- Does it give sensible results?
- Does it reason appropriately?
- Are its conclusions safe and useful?

Field testing

The decision aid will need to be tested in its intended environment:[2]

- Do users find it helpful?
- What effects does the system have on processes of health care delivery?
- Does the use of the system have a measurable effect on health outcome?

A number of different study designs can be used to test different aspects of these questions. The ideal design is a double-blind randomised controlled trial. The trial would involve the random allocation of patients, all of whom fulfil the definitions of the domain, either to a group in which the doctors use the decision aid or to a control group in which the doctors make their own unaided judgements. The patients would then be followed up for two purposes: first, to obtain sufficient evidence to make retrospective judgements about what the 'correct' answers should have been and, secondly, to make judgements about the outcomes that flowed from the decisions made—were the decisions worth making anyway? However, there are many potential biases in trials of decision aids (described by Wyatt and Spiegelhalter[2]): for example, the check-list effect will lead to improvement through more complete data collection during the trial.[6]

Maintenance and quality control

Knowledge in medicine changes, and populations in the domain on which the system is based may vary. Decision aids rest on the knowledge on and population for which they were developed, and they need regular review for quality control as does any laboratory test. Close attention to their use in centres away from the development site is required, with checks that the aid is being used on a similar population. If utilities are being gathered from patients to help decisions (see Chapters 9 and 10), the methodology of collecting the patients' opinions must be incorporated into the clinical routine. Thus, as with all decision support in medicine, from estimation of serum sodium to carotid angiography, a paper- or computer-supported decision aid requires regular maintenance.

Conclusion

This chapter presents an account of the effort (and years) that may be necessary to design, implement and evaluate a diagnostic decision aid for part of the neurological problem which is the theme of this book. The extent of the work that has gone into what is probably the most successful and extensively used decision aid for the diagnosis of acute abdominal pain shows that the difficulties involved are not over-emphasised.[7] One of the major problems is the time required to collect the data to build and maintain decision aids. However, the introduction of hospital information systems should make it possible for decision aids to be developed using the data collected routinely by these systems.[8] The power of organised routine collection of clinical data is illustrated by the use made of the Medicare data-base in the USA by Wennberg's group.[9]

Acknowledgement

Many of the ideas in this chapter were developed during collaborations with Jeremy Wyatt.

References

1. Duda RO, Gaschnig J, Hart PE, *et al. Development of the Prospector Consultation System for mineral exploration. Final Report, SRI Projects 5821 and 6451.* Menlo Park, CA: SRI International Inc, 1978
2. Wyatt J, Spiegelhalter D. Evaluating medical expert systems: what to test and how? *Medical Informatics* 1990; **15**: 205–17
3. Wyatt JC, Emerson PA. A pragmatic approach to knowledge engineering. In: Berry D, Hart A, eds. *Expert systems: human issues.* London: Chapman and Hall, 1990
4. Emerson PA, Wyatt JC, Dillistone L, Crichton N, Russell NJ. The development of ACORN, an expert system enabling nurses to make admission decisions about patients with chest pain in an accident and emergency department. In: *Proceedings of Medical Informatics Society,* September 1988
5. Wesson JH, Sox HC, Neff CK, Goldman L. Clinical prediction rules: applications and methodological standards. *New England Journal of Medicine* 1985; **313**: 793–9
6. Wyatt JC, Crichton NJ, Emerson PA. Computer assisted diagnosis of abdominal pain (letter). *British Medical Journal* 1986; **293**: 1305
7. de Dombal FT (and Project Steering Committee). *Computer aided diagnosis of acute abdominal pain; multicentre study, phase II Fund Report.* London: Department of Health and Social Security, 1985
8. Safran C, Herrmann F, Rind D, Kowaloff HB, Bleich HL, Slack WV. Computer-based support for clinical decision making. *MD Computing* 1990; **7**: 319–22
9. Barry MJ, Mulley AG, Fowler FJ, Wennberg JW. Watchful waiting vs immediate transurethral resection for symptomatic prostatism; the importance of patients' preferences. *Journal of the American Medical Association* 1988; **259**: 3010–7

9 | Practice guidelines and bringing the patient into clinical decisions

Anthony Hopkins*

Brook and Kosecoff write that good care implies:

> The performance of specific activities in a manner that either increases
> or at least prevents the deterioration in health status that would have
> occurred as a function of a disease or condition. Employing this definition,
> quality of care consists of two components (1) *the selection of the right
> activity or task* or (2) the performance of those activities in a manner that
> produces the best outcome.[1]

The words 'selection of the right activity' are stressed in italics
because selection means that decisions have to be made.

Donabedian, who has been pre-eminent in advancing our theoretical
understanding of medical audit, wrote in 1978 that the quality of
medical care was reflected in 'the degree of conformance to or deviation
from normative behaviour'.[2] In order to define the normative behaviour
of a physician, it is necessary to begin with the patient and his or her
perspective.

The patient's perspective

Physicians teach their students that patients do not present with
diseases or diagnoses, but with symptoms: that is, with disabilities or
handicaps in their everyday life. A patient states, for example, that he
gets a pain in his chest and is breathless on going upstairs. Immediately,
the physician has to make an initial assessment of the probabilities of
the various diagnoses that could account for these symptoms. The
point to make here is that the patient is interested primarily in his
symptoms and their potential relief. *All decision analysis must be directed
towards the achievement of outcomes that are valued by patients.* To take
a concrete example, Alonso has shown that drugs which improve the
expiratory outflow that can be achieved in one second in patients with
chronic obstructive airways disease (the FEV_1) do not necessarily
result in improvement in the patient's functional capacity.[3] There is a
simple but important lesson here. To continue with this example, there

*Director, Research Unit, Royal College of Physicians, London.

117

is no point in constructing an elegant clinical decision tree that encourages actions to improve the FEV_1 (a nice, easily measured value) if the patient continues with his existing symptoms. A decision tree has to be constructed simultaneously from root and most distal twig, the root being the symptoms with which the patient initially arrives, and the twigs being the outcomes which the patient hopes to achieve. The first role in clinical decision analysis therefore must be to define outcomes of value — of utility — to the individual patient. The next point is that it is no good defining an outcome which cannot be measured. The methods of estimating the utilities of the measured outcomes are outlined in Chapter 10.

Discordances between the patient's and medical perspectives

I believe that discordances between the patient's and medical perspectives on outcome account for many difficulties in everyday practice. To take the clinical example presented for discussion in Chapter 3 (the 70-year-old woman who has probably had a transient ischaemic attack), the outcome that *she* wants to achieve is a complete resolution of the clumsiness of the left hand. She also wants to be reassured that the clumsiness will not return. Many physicians are well aware that such vascular events often leave permanent residual neurological deficits. Neurologists will seem insensitive to their patients if they take that deficit as read, as it were, and concentrate upon aspects of clinical care that are seen to be of value to *them*—in this case therapy to lower blood pressure and appropriate treatment for the atrial fibrillation in order to prevent recurrence, as described in Chapter 6. Although a physician knows on the basis of randomised controlled trials that appropriate measures may reduce the possibilities of occurrence of stroke, he is also well aware that many patients with diffuse vascular disease will go on to have further vascular events whatever his intervention. He therefore has to be guarded in the prognosis that he gives this lady. She may then be dissatisfied on two counts: that the doctor can do nothing for her left hand (if a deficit in function had remained), and that he or she cannot say categorically that no further event will occur. This is a further outcome, in that the patient departs dissatisfied with the advice that she has received. Here, of course, is the need for of clinical skill in helping patients come to terms with illnesses for which it is often not possible to intervene effectively.

My main theme therefore is that it is important to re-examine the outcomes that doctors are attempting to achieve by their interventions, and to concentrate attention upon improvements of functional status and quality of life. Doctors should take an interest in biological markers of outcome only insofar as they reflect both that status and quality, and the probability of future pathological events that may cause a further deterioration.

Measurement of functional status

There is therefore a need to consider how best to measure both functional status and also patients' valuations of different functional statuses, in order to calculate more accurately the utilities at the end of the decision trees that are constructed. Fortunately, there have been considerable advances in the measurement of functional status in the last 20 years. Based upon their earlier work in the RAND Insurance Experiment, Ware and colleagues have developed a questionnaire with 36 questions (the SF-36) that has been shown in the Medical Outcomes Study reliably to distinguish between the health status of patients with a number of common diseases.[4] They have also shown that the question naire is responsive to changes in health status over time. There are considerable advantages in using a generic measure of health status such as this rather than disease-specific measures, not least because many medical patients are elderly and many have co-existent morbidities. For some disorders, such as rheumatoid arthritis, it may be better to choose a measure of health status which reflects the particular disabilities associated with that disorder. The best known example here is the Health Assessment Questionnaire (HAQ).[5] Many research studies use changes in HAQ questionnaire scores as a measure of outcome. To encourage the overall measure of functional status of older people, the Royal College of Physicians Research Unit, in conjunction with the British Geriatrics Society, has adopted the approach of choosing three or four of the number of readily available scales which measure functional ability in different domains. Our working group has recommended the Barthel Scale for physical disability, Hodkinson's Abbreviated Mental Test for mental function, the Philadelphia Geriatric Depression Scale for mood, and so on.[6] However, it has to be acknowledged that these scales are chosen because they measure aspects of health which are relatively easy to measure. The measurement of overall quality of life—what matters to the patient—is much more difficult. The best that can be done here at present is to concentrate on what are called 'health-related measures' of the quality of life, of which the SF-36 is one example.

There is, however, considerable research interest in developing methods which allow patients to describe their lives in terms of those factors which they consider to be important, rather than having an external system of dimensions of 'function' imposed upon them.[7,8]

With the efforts of the last two decades, therefore, there is no real difficulty in measuring functional status, but how can the values be estimated that patients put on the scores derived from these measures, and therefore the utility which should be attached to them in any decision tree? Efforts here are more vestigial, even though they also date back two decades to the original work of Rachel Rosser, in which she attempted to define the values that a sample of healthy people (albeit not representative of the general population) gave to different levels of disability and distress.[9]* There is an enormous research endeavour in attempting to value different health states. My view is that what is important is the individuality of the patient in terms of his or her own assessment of his or her quality of life. For example, a patient who is able to do most of what he or she wants in spite of a considerable physical disability such as paraplegia may enjoy a high quality of life, whereas another with minor symptoms scoring at a reasonable level on any scale of physical disability may be emotionally incapacitated by that impairment.

Practice guidelines

The importance of the patient's individuality in choosing the outcome that he or she most wishes to see leads to a central point in relation to the preparation of practice guidelines. Guidelines for good practice are designed to encourage the choice of procedures or therapies that have the most likelihood of achieving the defined outcome. These are crude instruments, but I believe them to be appropriate for disorders with a high mortality, or a high probability of a poor functional outcome resulting from an inappropriate choice. They are less relevant for those disorders in which the outcome valued by the patient will be largely chosen by the patient. Wennberg and his colleagues in the USA are particularly active in the field of assessing patient preferences in relation to whether or not prostatectomy should be undertaken. Their research studies using the Medicare data-base showed that the rate of incontinence and impotence after transurethral resection of the prostate was far higher than that reported in most of the clinical trials in centres of excellence.[11] A patient not much troubled by the need to get up at night several times to pass urine may well prefer to carry on doing this rather than run the risk of incontinence. Another patient may decide that the risk of impotence is, in his particular life, no longer of importance, and decide to have the operation. This is not to state that practice guidelines should *only* be used for disorders resulting in

*This topic forms the subject of a different publication in this series.[10]

mortality or a high chance of morbidity—outcomes which most, if not all, patients would hope to avoid—but that guidelines will necessarily become extremely complicated when there is a range of less severe possible outcomes, each of which might be differently valued by different patients.

In summary so far, the valuation of outcomes of therapeutic interventions may differ between patients. In a clinical decision tree, the nodes represent the choices between procedures, investigations or therapies that might be undertaken in any particular state. Clearly, the only paths to follow are those which have a reasonable probability of achieving the desirable outcome already defined. A definition of an effective treatment is one that has a high probability of achieving the desired outcome in a large proportion of those in that particular state.

Problems with practice guidelines

Unfortunately, patients vary not only in the values they attach to different outcomes, but also in the state in which they present. Randomised controlled trials have largely concealed this fact, because entry criteria are often so tight that the trial can give information only about the efficacy of a treatment in a small subgroup of the general population of those suffering with a particular disorder. Here then we come to *appropriateness*. A physician has to bear in mind not only the disorder suffered by the patient, and the valued outcome that patient hopes to achieve, but also the severity of the patient's present health state and other biological variables such as age and co-morbidities. All these factors will influence a physician's chances of achieving on the patient's behalf the outcome valued by the latter. The case for discussion (presented in Chapter 3) is a good example. Although the whole clinical problem lies within the general envelope of vascular disease, the presence of hypertension, mild hypercholesterolaemia and atrial fibrillation are all factors which need to be taken into account when choosing between various interventions in order to achieve the outcome valued by both patient and physician, which is a reduction in the chances of recurrence of a further vascular event.

For all the reasons advanced above, practice guidelines are comparatively blunt instruments. There is a further difficulty that, although guidelines are commonly written in terms of diagnoses, such as febrile convulsions, a urinary tract infection and so on, these largely beg the point. A febrile convulsion is a *discharge* diagnosis, not a *presenting* diagnosis. A child with meningitis and fever may well convulse, and any physician following a febrile convulsion protocol in this instance will have disastrous results if he or she fails to realise it is the wrong protocol to follow. Practice guidelines should therefore as far as possible be written in terms of presenting clinical problems rather than disease entities.

In spite of these reservations, the Research Unit is continuing to work with colleagues on the preparation of practice guidelines, as are many groups of physicians in individual hospitals in this country and, more particularly, in the USA. Criticisms directed at practice guidelines have largely been based upon the fact that they encourage 'cook book' medicine, this pejorative phrase presumably reflecting some of the anxieties formulated above. Other concerns are that they may be based upon current professional prejudice, which the passage of years will show to be unfounded. If they are to be credible, therefore, choice of therapies and procedures must be based upon the best available scientific evidence. Unfortunately, there is usually little interest in writing guidelines for the management of conditions in which the interventions are so dramatic that the benefits are self-evident. Instead, guidelines attempt to pick their way between the opposing camps of evidence that suggest on the one hand, such-and-such, and, on the other, this-and-that. The increasing realisation that work published in the best scientific journals remains of variable quality has led to the recent interest in meta-analysis, and the drawing up of 'rules of evidence'.[12,13]

There are further problems. The effect of the composition of the panel which writes the guidelines is relatively unrecognised. Persuasive advocates of a line of treatment can influence the final guidelines whatever the scientific evidence and, with the natural desire to achieve consensus, disparate views may be ignored or suppressed. Guidelines tend to be written largely by experts with great knowledge of biological aspects of the disease, and a decision tree may fail to reflect not only the perspective of the patients, but also the perspective of those working in primary care fields.

Attempts to involve patients in the production of guidelines have not, in my experience, been very successful. Individual patients can carry a perspective only slightly enlarged from their knowledge of their own illnesses. Representatives of patient organisations tend to be zealots, suggesting the expenditure of more resources and inappropriate investigations in an attempt to achieve valued outcomes. Bose and colleagues have drawn attention to Arrow's demonstration that no method by which a group chooses between alternatives can satisfy a number of reasonable conditions.[14] Simple majority voting procedures fail when more than two alternatives are being considered, and sequential majority voting is dependent upon the order in which binary choices are presented.[15] The paper by Bose *et al.* is no more than a mathematical reminder of a fact known to all hospital physicians, that the decision of a committee can be influenced by the choice of committee members, and by the order in which items on the agenda are presented.

Improvements to practice guidelines

One way in which practice guidelines could be greatly improved is by making choices explicit in the form of a decision tree. Outcomes should be defined, and a value attached to each, reflecting the values of a reasonable number of patients. (When the decision tree is applied to an individual patient, the tree must of course be recalculated using that individual's own valuations of the outcome.) The tree will also show the probability of achieving each outcome if a certain therapy is followed. Research evidence now allows a reasonable assessment of many probabilities, and there are better ways of measuring outcomes. The missing link is the value attached to those outcomes, and here a great deal more research is needed (see Chapter 10).

Conclusion

Research can, however, inform only in general about what people—and patients—value. In the individual clinical encounter, it is up to physicians to help their patients reach informed decisions, based upon their knowledge of the achievable outcomes, the probabilities of achieving them, and individual patient preferences and values. Only the physician and the patient together can reach this decision. This, it seems to me, is what used to be called 'clinical judgement'.

References

1. Brook RH, Kosecoff JB. Commentary: competition and quality. *Health Affairs* 1988; **7**: 150–61
2. Donabedian A. *Needed research in the assessment and monitoring of the quality of medical care. National Center for Health Services Research, Department of Health, Education and Welfare Publication No. (PHS)78–3219.* Washington: US DHEW, 1978
3. Alonso J, Anto JM, Gonzalez M, Fiz JA, Izquierdo J, Morera J. Measurement of general health status of non-oxygen-dependent chronic obstructive pulmonary disease patients. *Medical Care* 1992; **30** (suppl 5): MS125–35
4. Stewart AL, Greenfield S, Wells K, *et al*. Functional status and well-being of patients with chronic conditions: results from the Medical Outcomes Study. *Journal of the American Medical Association* 1989; **262**: 907–13

5. Fries JF, Spitz PW, Young DY. The dimensions of health outcomes: the Health Assessment Questionnaire, disability and pain scales. *Journal of Rheumatology* 1982; **9**: 789–93

6. *Standardised assessment scales for elderly people.* London: Royal College of Physicians Publications, 1992

7. Gerin P, Dazord A, Boissel J, Chifflet R. Quality of life assessment in therapeutic trials: rationale for and presentation of a more appropriate instrument. *Fundamental and Clinical Pharmacology* 1992; **6**: 263–76

8. McGee HM, O'Boyle CA, Hickey A, O'Malley K, Joyce CRB. Assessing the quality of life of the individual: the SEIQoL with a healthy and a gastroenterology unit population. *Psychological Medicine* 1991; **21**: 749–59.

9. Rosser RM, Kind P. A scale of valuations of states of illness — is there a social consensus? *International Journal of Epidemiology* 1978; **7**: 347–58

10. Hopkins A, ed. *Measures of the quality of life and the uses to which such measures may be put.* London: Royal College of Physicians Publications, 1993

11. Fowler FJ, Wennberg JE, Timothy RP, *et al.* Symptom status and quality of life following prostatectomy. *Journal of the American Medical Association* 1988; **259**: 3018–22

12. Mulrow CD. The medical review article: state of the science. *Annals of Internal Medicine* 1987; **104**: 485–8

13. Advisory Group on Health Technology Assessment. *Assessing the effects of health technologies: principles, practice, proposals, 10/91 5M.* London: Department of Health, 1992

14. Bose DK, Heathfield HA, Andrew M. Collective decision problems in medicine — a basic approach looking for cross-fertilization in clinical surgery. *Theoretical Surgery* 1992; **7**: 186–93

15. Arrow KJ. *Social choice and individual values.* New York: John Wiley, 1963

10 | Estimating utilities for making decisions in health care

Michael Drummond*

Decisions are made at a number of different levels in the health care sector. In determining overall health care policies, the decisions are being made for the whole population. In clinical decision making, decisions are being made for individual patients. The two decision making spheres are not totally independent of each other since some of the broader health policy decisions shape the environment in which the clinician is working. However, both sets of decisions have consequences for the allocation of health care resources.

In both decision making spheres there is a need to assess the valuations that individuals place on health states. First, in clinical decision analysis, data on the patient's values are combined, either formally or informally, with data on the probabilities of clinical outcomes in order to select the preferred course of treatment. Secondly, in making health care policy, it is useful to have data on the value of health care treatments and programmes in order to compare with their costs. The reason for wanting to assess health state valuations may determine how they are obtained, for example, whom to ask. However, the literature on health state valuations does not in general make such clear distinctions. Professionals from a number of disciplines have contributed to this literature, including clinical researchers, epidemiologists, psychologists, medical sociologists, operational researchers and health economists.

This chapter will review the literature, and address the following issues:

- What methods are used to obtain valuations of health states?

- What valuations are obtained, in particular relating to health states relevant to the clinical management of an individual having a transient ischaemic attack (TIA) (the illustrative condition used in this book)?

- What are the current methodological debates surrounding the valuation of health states?

- What issues are raised by the use of valuations of health states in making clinical decisions or health care policies?

*Centre for Health Economics, University of York.

Methods for obtaining valuations of health states

The objective of all the measurement methods is to yield a single value, often called a 'utility' value, for given states of health on an interval scale. The scale is usually standardised so that dead is equal to 0 and perfect health to 1 (or 100). However, some states of health have been rated by respondents as being 'worse than death' and are represented by negative values.[1] Therefore, when individuals' valuations are elicited it is now customary to refer to 'best' and 'worst' possible health states without making a prior judgement about where dead would fall on the scale. Valuations can be obtained from individuals concerning their own current state of health or other health states which are described to them in various ways.

The term 'utility', as used in the health state valuation literature, has its origins in the theory of rational decision making developed by von Neumann and Morgenstern.[2] Torrance and Feeny note that it is doubly unfortunate that those authors called their new approach 'utility theory' and the associated preference measures 'utilities'.[3] First, in their usage, utility did not mean usefulness as it does in normal language and, secondly, it meant neither what it traditionally meant to economists and philosophers during the nineteenth century nor what it means to modern economists. It is therefore better to treat the valuations obtained as 'health state preferences' rather than as 'utilities'.

Measurement of utilities

Direct measurement

Three main methods of measurement have emerged: the rating scale, the time trade-off approach and the standard gamble.

A typical *rating scale* consists of a line on a page with clearly defined end-points. The most preferred health state is placed at one end of the line and the least preferred at the other end. The remaining health states lie between these two, such that the intervals or spacing between them correspond to the differences in preference as perceived by the person (the subject) placing states on the line. For example, the subject may be asked to select the best health state of a batch of descriptions concerning restrictions of activity, pain and so on, and the worst, which may or may not be death. He or she is then asked to locate the other states on the scale, such that the distances between the locations are proportional to the subject's differences in preference. The rating scale is measured between 0 and 1. If death is judged to be the worst state and placed at the 0 end of the rating scale, the preference value for each of the other states is the scale value of its location. If death is not judged to be the worst state but is placed at some intermediate point on the scale, say, d, the preference values of the other states are given by the formula $(x - d)/(1 - d)$, where x is the scale location of the health state. In some studies, more sophisticated 'props' are now being used to aid the respondent, such as 'health thermometers'.

In the *time trade-off* approach the respondent is asked to consider the relative amounts of time he would be willing to spend in various health states. For example, in order to value a chronic health state, the respondent would be offered a choice of remaining in this state for the rest of his life versus returning to complete health for a shorter period. The amount of time the individual is willing to 'trade' to return to perfect health can be used to obtain a preference value for the chronic health state. A similar approach can be used to calculate the relative values of temporary health states.

The time trade-off method was developed by Torrance et al.[4] Preferences for temporary health states can be measured as shown in Fig. 1. As with the other scales, intermediate states i are measured relative to the best state (healthy) and the worst state (temporary state j). The subject is offered two alternatives:

- temporary state i for time t (the time duration specified for the temporary state), followed by healthy;
- temporary state j for time $x < t$, followed by healthy.

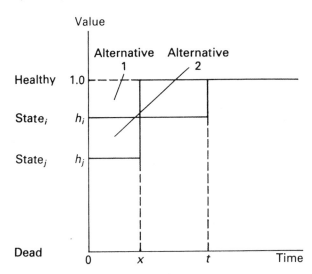

Fig. 1. *Time trade-off for a temporary health state.*

Time x is varied until the respondent is indifferent between the two alternatives, at which point the value for state i, $h_i = 1 - (1 - h_j)x/t$. With $h_j = 0$, $h_i = 1 - x/t$.

The *standard gamble* is the classical method of measuring preferences, based directly on the fundamental axioms of utility theory. In order to measure preferences for chronic states preferred to death, the subject is offered two alternatives, either the gamble, a treatment with two possible outcomes (death or return to normal health for the remainder of his life), or the certain outcome of remaining in the chronic state for the rest of his life. The probability of a successful outcome to the gamble is varied until the respondent is indifferent between the gamble and the certainty. This probability can then be used to calculate the preference value for the health state. The method can be illustrated by the weights to be assigned to *temporary* health states where h is an index of health as illustrated in Fig. 2. Slightly different approaches are used to assess states worse than death and chronic health states.

The subject is offered two alternatives:

- a procedure with two outcomes: normal health, h_h, with probability p, or the worst state h_j, with probability $1 - p$; or
- some intermediate health state, h_i.

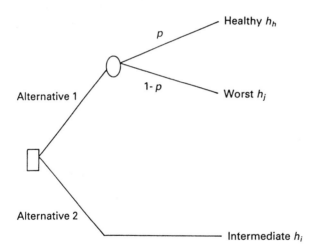

Fig. 2. *Standard gamble for a temporary health state.*

Given initial arbitrary numbers assigned to h_h and h_j ($h_h > h_j$), the subject is offered alternative probabilities until he or she becomes indifferent between the two alternatives, at which point:

$$h_i = p + (1 - p)h_j$$

As with the rating scale, various 'props' have been designed to help respondents interpret the choices in the time-off and the standard gamble. This is particularly important for the standard gamble where individuals may have difficulty understanding probabilities. One frequently used prop is the 'chance board', which depicts the probabilities as slices of a pie chart.[5]

Although some of the approaches to health state valuation appear complicated, they are relatively easy to carry out in an interview with the respondent. In research studies at least, the cost of obtaining health state valuations is not a major impediment to the application of the approach. The practicalities of undertaking valuations as part of making clinical decisions or health care policies are discussed later.

Pre-scaled utility measures

It would be ideal to undertake direct measurements of all relevant health states for all relevant individuals, but this would be a mammoth task. Therefore, for applications related to making health care policy (as opposed to making clinical decisions) it has become popular to use pre-scaled utility measures, generic measures upon which any health state can be located, and which have been derived using the valuations of a given sample of individuals. The most widely used measure of this type in the UK is that developed by Kind *et al.* (see Table 1).[6] The

Table 1. Valuation matrix for 70 respondents.

| | Distress rating | | | |
| | A | B | C | D |
Disability rating	No distress	Mild	Moderate	Severe
1. No disability	1.000	0.995	0.990	0.967
2. Slight social disability	0.990	0.986	0.973	0.932
3. Severe social disability and/or slight physical impairment	0.980	0.972	0.956	0.912
4. Physical ability severely limited (eg light housework only)	0.964	0.956	0.942	0.870
5. Unable to take paid employment or education, largely housebound	0.946	0.935	0.900	0.700
6. Confined to chair or wheelchair	0.875	0.845	0.680	0.000
7. Confined to bed	0.677	0.564	0.000	−1.486
8. Unconscious	−1.078	*	*	*

Source: Kind *et al.*[6]
1.0 = healthy
0.0 = dead
* = not applicable

notion is that any health state can be described by a particular combination of the two dimensions of disability and distress. The number in the relevant cell of the matrix represents the utility value for the health state.

In addition to the Rosser-Kind index, three other pre-scaled measures are worth mentioning:

1. The Torrance Multi-attribute Utility Function.[7] This has four dimensions which allow utility values for 960 health states to be derived:
   - physical function (mobility and physical activity);
   - role function (self-care and role activity);
   - social-emotional function (emotional well-being and social activity); and
   - health problem.

2. The General Well-Being Scale.[8] This was derived using a rating scale technique on the general public in San Diego. It has subsequently been replicated in other groups, including sufferers from arthritis, to assess the reproducibility of the valuations of health states obtained. It has been widely used in the USA.

3. The EuroQol[c]. This measure has been developed in an international collaborative effort, and has been tested on populations in a number of countries.[9] At the time of the pilot study, it had six dimensions:
   - mobility;
   - self-care;
   - main activity;
   - social relationships;
   - pain; and
   - mood.

The appeal of the generic pre-scaled measures is obvious in the case of making health care policy where decisions are being made for groups of individuals. However, while it has been found that the average valuations of health states for groups of individuals in the population are relatively similar,[10] valuations of a given health state are known to vary widely between individuals. In making clinical decisions, however, the choice is being made for a particular patient, as is stressed in Chapter 9, and it is difficult to see how it is possible to proceed without eliciting valuations of the relevant health state for that individual through direct measurement.

Expert opinion

One possible way to proceed would be through the use of expert opinion; those with extensive experience of a particular health state could suggest a valuation. The experts have normally been physicians. There are some examples of this approach in the literature, but again these are usually applications relating to health care policy making. For example, Stason and Weinstein considered that a person suffering side-effects from antihypertensive medicines would have a health state valued at 0.99 or 0.97.[11] They then considered the impact that differing assumptions about the valuation of health states would have on their analysis.

In applications relating to making clinical decisions, the use of expert opinion for valuations of health states is obviously linked to issues such as informed consent and the extent to which the patient wishes the physician to act as his or her agent. Few, if any, researchers advocate the use of experts' values, except possibly to introduce the patient to the concept before proceeding to elicit his or her own valuations.

Valuations of health states reported in the literature

Table 2 gives health state utilities from a general population sample obtained by Torrance *et al.* using the time trade-off technique.[4] Three features are worth noting. First, in each case a high percentage of the responses were usable, indicating that, despite the apparent complexity of the questions posed, individuals are willing and able to participate. (In general, the levels of refusals and broken-off interviews are low.) However, interviewing patients raises additional issues: on the one hand, it can be viewed as a natural extension of informed consent but, on the other, it may induce unnecessary anxiety. Therefore, if undertaken as part of a research project, such interviews should be considered as an intervention and subject to ethical approval.

Secondly, the values that individuals place on health states are not independent of the time in those states. (This is an important point and will be returned to later.) Thirdly, the standard errors in Table 2 indicate the large degree of variability in individuals' assessments of health states.

Unfortunately, there are few valuations of health states reported in the literature relating to the clinical options for the management of TIAs, the condition outlined for consideration in Chapter 3. For example, although there have been a number of quality of life studies in the field of antihypertensive therapy, these are mostly descriptive in nature.[13] The most widely known health state valuations are the judgements made by Stason and Weinstein cited above.[11]

Table 2. Mean daily health state utilities in the general population sample.

Duration	Health state	Observations		Mean daily health state utility	Standard error
		Total	Usable		
	Reference state: perfect health			1.00	
3 months	Home confinement for tuberculosis	246	239	0.68	0.020
3 months	Home confinement for an unnamed contagious disease	246	240	0.65	0.022
3 months	Hospital dialysis	246	243	0.62	0.023
3 months	Hospital confinement for tuberculosis	246	241	0.60	0.022
3 months	Hospital confinement for an unnamed contagious disease	246	242	0.56	0.023
3 months	Depression	246	243	0.44	0.024
8 years	Home dialysis	246	240	0.65	0.018
8 years	Mastectomy for injury	60	56	0.63	0.038
8 years	Kidney transplant	246	242	0.58	0.021
8 years	Hospital dialysis	246	240	0.56	0.019
8 years	Mastectomy for breast cancer	60	58	0.48	0.044
8 years	Hospital confinement for an unnamed contagious disease	246	241	0.33	0.022
life	Home dialysis	197	187	0.40	0.031
life	Hospital dialysis	197	189	0.32	0.028
life	Hospital confinement for an unnamed contagious disease	197	192	0.16	0.020
	Reference state: dead			0.00	
	Total	3,171	3,093		

Source: Drummond *et al.*[12]

Preliminary estimates can be obtained from the pre-scaled generic utility scales. For example, the health state valuation of 0.986 is given by the Rosser-Kind matrix for the state 'slight social disability with mild distress'. (This might correspond to someone such as our illustrative patient on long-term medication experiencing side-effects.) Alternatively, someone suffering a disabling stroke might be 'confined to chair or wheelchair with moderate distress'. This state has a value of 0.680 on the matrix. Such estimates are inevitably crude due to the broad nature of the Rosser-Kind classifications. Therefore, to progress with the analysis of this particular clinical problem, further investigation would be required, either by eliciting particular patients' values in a clinical decision analysis, or by asking a representative sample of the general public for their valuations to inform health care policy decisions.

Current methodological debates

Do evaluations of health states represent true utilities?

First, it has already been pointed out that valuations of health states do not represent 'utilities' in the classic economic sense. Secondly, Mooney and Olsen have argued that there is more to the utility of health care than that derived from the health state itself.[14] For example, there is an informational content in making health care decisions which is of value to the patient. There is some empirical evidence to support this point. In a survey of patients' willingness to pay for the components of information contained in an ultrasound examination during apparently normal pregnancies, Berwick and Weinstein found that 40% of those patients willing to pay would pay for the information even if the physician were unable to learn the results and, therefore, could not alter decisions accordingly, and 29% of the value was unrelated to the ability of either the physician *or* the patient to alter subsequent actions on the basis of the information.[15] This value lay in 'just knowing' whether, for example, the fetus was healthy, was due within three months, or was or was not twins. Mooney and Olsen argue that more research is required to determine how to incorporate these and any other factors that the patient wants included into the patient's utility function.[14]

Which measurement method should be used?

It is well-known that the different measurement methods (rating scale, time trade-off and standard gamble) yield different results. Values for the standard gamble are typically higher than those for the other two.

The standard gamble has most advocates, being most closely aligned to the original von Neumann and Morgenstern methodology. Until recently, it suffered from practical problems in administration relating to difficulties in respondents interpreting probabilities, but these seem to have been solved by the development of superior props such as the 'chance board'.[5]

The main difference between the standard gamble and the other approaches is that it introduces risk. Many people appear to be risk-averse when faced with a choice of a certain period of survival (in years) and entering into a gamble with a 50% probability of dying and a 50% probability of surviving for (say) 20 years. A risk-neutral person would opt for a certain period of ten years, which is the expected value (in years) of the gamble. Anyone opting for less than that would be risk-averse, discounting the future, reflecting a diminishing marginal value of additional years of life, or all three. This notion was first explored in the medical field by McNeil *et al.*[16]

It has been argued that there is no reason to exclude individuals' risk preferences when using health state valuations for making health care policy.[14] In making clinical decisions, the position is less clear. First, there is the rather confusing situation that the standard gamble is itself usually depicted in terms of clinical choices, whereas its real purpose is to elicit the health state valuation. Secondly, the health state valuations (which, if estimated by the standard gamble, may have some element of risk preference) are then used in a clinical decision analysis combined with probabilities to calculate expected values for the treatment options. This potentially gives the patient a second opportunity to introduce his risk preference if there is further debate. Therefore, the practical significance of introducing valuations of health states with risk preferences into clinical decision analysis requires more discussion. Presumably, the correct approach would be not to enter into further debate, but to present to the patient the clinical decision tree, showing the treatment choice that would be preferred, given the health state valuations previously estimated.

On the other hand, there may be problems with valuations of health states obtained by the time trade-off approach if the value of a state is not independent of the time spent in the state. In the time trade-off, the respondent is asked to choose between two certainties, and the indifference point sought between t years in an inferior (chronic) health state and x years in perfect health. When the indifference point is revealed, the researcher assigns a utility value equivalent to x/t, which is assumed to be constant through the t years. However, various researchers have argued that an individual's valuation of a given state may change through time. If the state is not too severe, the patient may learn to cope more easily, whereas an inferior state may impose an increasing burden if experienced for a longer time. (This is one interpretation of the data in Table 2.)

These problems have led some researchers to question the wisdom of constructing quality-adjusted life years (QALYs) by multiplying health state valuations by the time spent in the state (see Fig. 3). Mehrez and Gafni have proposed an alternative measure called the 'healthy-years equivalent',[17] which is not too dissimilar in concept from the certainty equivalents proposed by McNeil *et al.*[16] There are a number of reasons to suppose that this measure is theoretically superior to the QALY, although there are important measurement implications. The healthy-years equivalent measure requires the complete profile of health states into the future for each disease to be specified, and the individual then asked to undertake a standard gamble. This would be time-consuming if a number of profiles need to be evaluated.

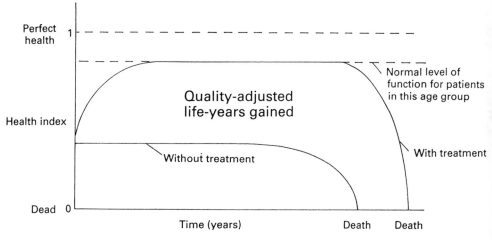

Fig. 3. *Quality-adjusted life years added by treatment.*

Finally, no matter which measurement method is used, it is important to be aware that valuations may be affected by the way in which the question is asked. The most well-known of the 'framing effects' is that first alluded to by Kahneman and Tversky.[18] Basically, different answers are obtained in a standard gamble, in terms of death or survival, depending on whether probabilities are presented. There may be other subtle influences of the way in which choices are posed. Llewellyn-Thomas *et al.* noticed that the values obtained from a group of raters for a series of health states (using the standard gamble) were strongly influenced by characteristics of the 'failure' outcome of the gamble.[19] Raters were prepared to bear a greater risk in the gamble when death was the 'worst' outcome. The authors went on to argue that if attempts are to be made to assess an individual patient's values with the standard gamble in the context of a clinical decision, it would seem reasonable to include death as an outcome in the gamble where this was a possible outcome of the clinical situation under consideration, but to omit death where this was not a possibility and to substitute the worst possible alternative clinical outcome.

Practical issues in using health state valuations

Clinical decision making

One clear implication of what has been said so far is that in making decisions for a particular patient, the individual person's valuations should be used (as also described in Chapter 9). Because of the wide variations in valuations of health states, it is unlikely that other people's values (including those of the patient's physician) will suffice. Indeed, there is evidence from two studies in the cancer field that there is sometimes little agreement between doctors and patients on the assessment of the patient's quality of life and the aims of therapy.[20,21] However, other people's values might be used in order to introduce the patient to the concepts. Even here the issues are not entirely clear. Christensen-Szalanski found that women preferred to avoid using anaesthesia during childbirth when asked one month before labour and during early labour.[22] However, during later stages of labour their preference shifted towards avoiding pain, a view which prevailed one month post partum. Which set of preferences is the most relevant? One approach would be for the clinician to point out to the patient that many individuals' preferences change in the way outlined. Also, it is possible to use videos to explain to a patient how other people feel— which has been explored in the USA in relation to health states after prostatectomy.

Another implication, although perhaps more subject to debate, is that the standard gamble or its variant, the 'certainty equivalent' used by McNeil et al.[16] is the preferred method of eliciting valuations of health states for clinical decisions. In particular, it is important to have a method that considers choice under uncertainty and in which risk preferences can be introduced.

Other implications are less obvious and require further discussion. First, it is not clear how to introduce other factors that are not traditionally considered. These include the value of information, the utility asociated with the *process* of care rather than with its outcome, and the regret and rejoicing associated with decision making. (This last aspect has been explored by, among others, Loomes and Sugden, and has been offered as one explanation why there are disparities between different health state measures.[23,24]) As Weinstein has said: 'it is clearly naive to assume that patients wish to maximise quality-adjusted life expectancy—but what do they wish to maximise?'[25]

Secondly, it is important to understand how the framing of the question and other factors (such as whether or not 'dead' is included as a failure of the gamble) impact upon patients' choices in a standard gamble. It should also be noted that the clinician can introduce a framing effect by describing given health states in either a positive or a negative way.

Finally, an assessment needs to be made of whether the decomposition of the decision into elements of probabilities and outcomes (in terms of health states) is really helpful. The holistic decision of whether or not to undergo an operation may sometimes be easier to confront than the kinds of choices presented in the classical health state valuation exercises. (These issues are debated further by Dowie.[26]) In the context of making clinical decisions, the objective of the approaches outlined above should be the improvement of decision making for the individual patient. Some patients may welcome more information and increased participation in treatment choices, and others may not. Therefore, it is not necessarily the case that more analysis helps in every situation.

Making health care policy

There has been considerable interest in the use of valuations of health states to inform decisions about policy. The recent economics literature has centred on the use of the QALY as a generic output measure and on the construction of 'league tables' of health care interventions in terms of their cost per QALY gained (see Table 3). Many economists, most notably Williams,[27] have argued that such league tables can assist policy makers in assigning priorities for the allocation of resources. In the UK, the most frequently used utility values have been those derived by Kind et al.[6] (shown in Table 1). These can be combined with prognostic data on the likely course of the disease, with or without treatment, from clinical trials or expert opinion to derive the kind of diagram shown in Fig. 3. In North America, effort has concentrated on obtaining direct measurements from individuals for a wide range of health states.[10]

The use of cost per QALY league tables has been a source of heated debate.[2] First, it has been argued that the mortality and morbidity data upon which QALY calculations are based are not sufficiently precise.

Table 3. 'League table' of costs and quality-adjusted life years for selected health care interventions (1983/4 prices).*

Intervention	Present value of extra cost per QALY gained (£)
GP advice to stop smoking	170
Pacemaker implantation for heart block	700
Hip replacement	750
CABG for severe angina LMD	1040
GP control of total serum cholesterol	1700
CABG for severe angina with 2VD	2280
Kidney transplantation (cadaver)	3000
Breast cancer screening	3500
Heart transplantation	5000
CABG for mild angina 2VD	12600
Hospital haemodialysis	14000

Adapted from: Williams[27]
CABG = coronary artery bypass graft
GP   = general practitioner
LMD = left mainstem arterial disease
QALY = quality-adjusted life year
2VD   = two-vessel disease

*Inflate figures by 60% to obtain approximate 1993 prices.

However, the supporters of QALYs argue that, notwithstanding their problems, these data are the best available for decision making, and that their use in this way may stimulate epidemiologists and clinical researchers to improve upon them.

Secondly, it has been pointed out that the different utility methods yield different results, an issue that merits further investigation. In the meantime, it would be important to assess, through sensitivity analyses, whether health utility values *do* have a critical influence on study results. It may be that the results are just as sensitive to other estimates, such as those of costs. In situations where the utility values are critical, as they clearly are in the illustration in Chapter 3, the analyst can only make this explicit and leave it to the decision maker to come to his or her own conclusions about the validity and reliability of the estimation methods used.

Thirdly, it has been noted that many of the cost per QALY values reported in the literature are average values, whereas the real choices are at the margins. For example, it can be seen in Table 3 that pacemaker implantation is near the top of the league, and is therefore a strong candidate for expansion. However, the cost per QALY of the next stage in the expansion of use of pacemaker technology may not be the same as that reported there. For example, the pacemakers required for the extra patients may be more sophisticated in design, and consequently more costly. Furthermore, it is likely that the patients who would be treated in the next expansion of pacemaker technology are less seriously ill than those who have already been implanted. Therefore, the benefits of treatment would be slightly lower. However, Table 3, and some of the other tables reported, embody margins to the extent that expansions in the indications for therapy are considered (eg from severe angina with left mainstem arterial disease to moderate angina with two-vessel disease). Consideration of these margins, and the resulting costs and QALYs, would be relevant for the clinicians concerned to decide upon their treatment priorities, given limited resources.

Fourthly, it has been argued that the highly summarised presentation of data in one cost per QALY estimate is dangerous in that it suggests quick and easy solutions to the decision maker.[28] This is an important point and, to the extent that they encourage *less* thought by decision makers about the difficulty and complexity of health care choices, these league tables may be counterproductive. For example, is the decision maker happy to accept that a gain of one year of healthy life is equivalent to a gain of 0.1 in utility for each of ten years? Are gains in length of life and quality of life different attributes that should be presented separately? Because of these and other complexities, it is the responsibility of economic analysts to continue to stress that such estimates are only an *aid* to decision making, not a substitute for thought.

Fifthly, some commentators have suggested that broad comparisons across widely different medical fields are unwise. Of course these choices have to be made, indeed *are* made, through the policy process in health care. The question is therefore again one of whether such analysis helps those making the choices. In addition, it should be noted that many of the cost per QALY league tables also address choices *within* given clinical fields, such as open heart surgery and angioplasty, as well as between different branches of medicine. Another way forward would be to consider the costs and QALYs of different interventions for a given care group, such as the elderly or children, on the grounds that the allocation of a budget for the care of the group concerned would have already been made through the political process and that the main question is how best to use the budget.

A sixth objection is that the strict application of the cost per QALY league table would imply that some groups in society, whose treatment has a high cost per QALY, would receive no care. Of course it is true that the decision rule being applied is one that would maximise the total amount of health (as measured by QALYs), given the resources available. That is, it is concerned with economic efficiency rather than with notions of equity or justice in the distribution of health care resources. Society may take the view that it wishes to give everyone an equal chance of receiving care no matter with what condition they are suffering. However, this view needs to be examined critically, since at the limit it would imply that two individuals, one suffering from an incurable condition and another suffering from an easily curable one, should receive equal access to treatment, even though the chances of success are zero in one case and high in the other. Perhaps there are better ways in which society could exercise its moral duty, by giving access to palliative care and psychological help to those suffering from terminal illness, rather than engaging in heroic, unproven therapy. This does not however deny the need for more medical research in such cases, provided that it is carried out in accordance with a well reasoned research protocol. It should also be remembered that the cost per QALY league table embodies a kind of equality, in that a QALY is considered to be worth the same to every individual. These ethical aspects of using QALYs are discussed particularly in reference 28.

A seventh point, also linked to research, is that the cost per QALY estimates relate to treatment interventions at a particular stage in their development. Technological advances may make some of the interventions much more attractive in the future, and these advances may never be realised if the treatments are discontinued. Certainly, the cost per QALY estimates should be continually updated to take account of technological advances, and research should continue to take place into all developing treatments. It is not wise, however, to continue funding interventions that give poor value for money merely in the anticipation of future technological advances; equally, technological advances in other, competing fields may make them even less worthwhile in the future. Nevertheless, the calculation of costs and QALYs helps indicate situations in which technological advances would potentially generate large benefits.

Finally, it was mentioned above that the methods of measurement in fact measure utility in the strictest economic sense. It was also suggested that it might be wise therefore to view these measures merely as preferences for health states rather than as true utilities, and to regard the construction of QALYs not as a method of measuring the total utility gains from health care interventions but as a way of making the difficult trade-offs of length and quality of life more explicit. There-fore, the value of the approach rests on whether or not decision makers make better resource allocation decisions if given this information. For example, the appropriate use of the information in Table 3 is not necessarily to cease treatment for kidney dialysis patients. It is rather to discourage health authorities from cutting back on high value-for-money treatments like hip replacement in the interests of short-run political expediency, and to stimulate further debate among cardio-vascular surgeons on the appropriate indications for coronary artery bypass grafting versus angioplasty or medical treatment.

Despite the methodological and practical difficulties of output measure-ment in health care, such measures are clearly required for decisions about allocating resources. The alternative, of relying on measures of mortality, or throughput measures such as 'cases treated', is far from satisfactory. Therefore, policy makers need to use the available measures intelligently, whilst simultaneously encouraging research into their refinement.

In considering the use of the available measures, QALYs, despite their problems, have undoubted attractions, and policy makers should encourage the production of data on the costs and QALYs gained from health care interventions. However, care should be taken in interpreting the results, given the methodological differences between studies and the concerns over whether this approach fully reflects all the relevant dimensions of choice at the societal level, in particular aspects of equity. The production of cost and QALY values should be viewed as a way of asking questions about the resource consequences of interventions and their contribution to length and quality of life, not as the sole basis for decision making.

Conclusion

In the field of health care, decisions are made both in determining health care policy and in selecting the preferred course of treatment for the individual patient. In both decision making spheres there is a need to assess the valuations that individuals place on health states. A number of methods exist to elicit these valuations, or health 'utilities'. Each method has its advantages and disadvantages, but an important feature of the standard gamble approach is that it incorporates indivi-duals' attitudes to risk. There are few health state valuations reported in the literature relating to the clinical options for the management of TIAs (the illustrative condition of interest). However, preliminary estimates can be obtained from pre-scaled generic utility scales. There are a number of current methodological debates, including whether valuations of health states represent true utilities, and which measurement methods should be used. The use of these valuations in making clinical and health policy decisions also raises a number of important practical issues and issues relating to equity and the allocation of resources.

References

1. Boyle MH, Torrance GW, Sinclair JC, *et al*. Economic evaluation of neonatal intensive care of very-low-birth-weight infants. *New England Journal of Medicine* 1983; **308**: 1330–7

2. von Neumann J, Morgenstern O. *Theory of games and economic behaviour*. Princeton, NJ: Princeton University Press, 1944

3. Torrance GW, Feeny D. Utilities and quality-adjusted life-years. *International Journal of Technology Assessment in Health Care* 1989; **5**: 559–75

4. Torrance GW, Thomas WH, Sackett DL. A utility maximization model for evaluation of health care programs. *Health Services Research* 1972; **7**: 118–33

5. Furlong W, Feeny D, Torrance GW, *et al*. *Guide to design and development of health-state utility instrumentation. Centre for Health Economics and Policy Analysis Working Paper 90–9*. Hamilton, Ontario: McMaster University, 1991

6. Kind P, Rosser RM, Williams AH. Valuation of quality of life: some psychometric evidence. In: Jones-Lee MW, ed. *The value of life and safety*. Amsterdam: Elsevier/North Holland, 1982

7. Torrance GW, Boyle MH, Horwood SP. Application of multi-attribute utility theory to measure social preferences for health states. *Operations Research* 1982; **30**: 1043–69

8. Kaplan RM, Bush JW, Berry CC. Health status: types of validity and the index of well-being. *Health Services Research* 1976; **11**: 478–507

9. EuroQol^c Group. EuroQol^c—a new facility for the measurement of health-related quality of life. *Health Policy* 1990; **16**: 199–208

10. Torrance GW. Utility approach to measuring health-related quality of life. *Journal of Chronic Diseases* 1987; **40**: 593–600

11. Stason WB, Weinstein MC. Allocation of resources to manage hypertension. *New England Journal of Medicine* 1977; **296**: 732–9

12. Drummond MF, Stoddart GL, Torrance GW. *Methods for the economic evaluation of health care programmes*. Oxford: Oxford University Press, 1987

13. Drummond MF, Teeling Smith G, Wells N. *Economic evaluation in the development of medicines*. London: Office of Health Economics, 1988

14. Mooney G, Olsen, JA. QALYs: where next? In: McGuire A, Fenn P, Mayhew K, eds. *Providing health care*. Oxford: Oxford University Press, 1991

15. Berwick DM, Weinstein MC. What do patients value? Willingness to pay for ultrasound in normal pregnancy. *Medical Care* 1985; **23**: 881–93

16. McNeil BJ, Weichselbaum R, Pauker SG. Fallacy of the five-year survival in lung cancer. *New England Journal of Medicine* 1978; **299**: 1397–1401

17. Mehrez A, Gafni A. Quality-adjusted life years, utility theory and healthy-years equivalents. *Medical Decision Making* 1989; **9**: 142–9
18. Kahneman D, Tversky A. Prospect theory: an analysis of decision under risk. *Econometrica* 1979; **47**: 263–91
19. Llewellyn-Thomas H, Sutherland HJ, Tibshirani R, *et al.* The measurement of patients' values in medicine. *Medical Decision Making* 1982; **2**: 449–62
20. Slevin ML, Plant H, Lynch D, *et al.* Who should measure quality of life, the doctor or the patient? *British Journal of Cancer* 1988; **57**: 109–12
21. Maher EJ, Goodman S, Jefferis A. Decision-making in the management of advanced cancer of head and neck. Differences in perspective between doctors and patients: future avenues for research. *Palliative Medicine* 1990; **4**: 185–9
22. Christensen-Szalanski JJJ. Discount functions and the measurement of patients' values: women's decisions during childbirth. *Medical Decision Making* 1984; **4**: 47–58
23. Loomes G, Sugden R. Regret theory: an alternative theory of rational choice under uncertainty. *Economic Journal* 1982; **92**: 805–24
24. Loomes G. *Disparities between health state measures: an explanation and some implications.* Paper presented to the Health Economists' Study Group. Brunel University, July 1988
25. Weinstein MC. Risky choices in medical decision making. *The Geneva Papers on Risk and Insurance* 1976; **11**: 197–216
26. Dowie J. *Professional judgement: introductory text: 7. Valuing outcomes.* Milton Keynes: The Open University, 1988
27. Williams AH. Economics of coronary artery bypass grafting. *British Medical Journal* 1985; **291**: 326–9
28. Hopkins A, ed. *Measures of the quality of life—and the uses to which such measures may be put.* London: Royal College of Physicians of London Publications, 1992

11 | Decision analysis in the context of day-to-day clinical practice, audit and research

Huw Llewelyn*

Most diagnoses and decisions in day-to-day clinical practice have to be made quickly and the reasoning process is often subconscious. For example, most doctors would recognise immediately that a patient who had suddenly developed limb and facial weakness, which was also resolving rapidly, had probably suffered a transient cerebral ischaemic attack (TIA). Many doctors would think it impracticable to try to use decision analysis, algorithms or expert systems to solve clinical problems of this kind in busy wards and clinics. However, it is easy to understand how mistakes happen in these circumstances and why it might be a good idea to use formal methods of interpreting information during some kind of checking process. Medical audit in its present form takes place retrospectively and therefore happens too late to allow errors to be corrected before they can cause harm. The best that can be done is to use the findings of audit to try to prevent similar mistakes happening in the future. What is needed is a method of checking decisions quickly before they are implemented.

Analysing, explaining and checking decisions

After deciding what is to be done, the modern doctor is usually obliged to fill in a form which will require a response from other doctors, pharmacists, biochemists, chemical pathologists, radiologists, nurses and/or physiotherapists who will usually expect an explanation for what they are being asked to do. Before such an explanation can be provided it is necessary to reflect on the decision and thus analyse it to some extent. The decision would thus also undergo a checking process. If the explanation is to be provided formally using a computer system, it is important to be clear about how this analysis and explanation should be conducted. It is also important to understand the difference

*School of Medicine and Dentistry, King's College, London.

between—and be able to distinguish—those situations for which the quantitative form of clinical decision analysis (sometimes given initial capitals) described elsewhere in this book is appropriate and the other, simpler situations for which the 'clinical decision analysis' (without capitals) is more basic but applicable to all decisions.

The simplest form of analysis would be, first, to recall the diagnosis that was the indication for the request (usually a differential diagnosis if it was for a test) and then to describe the clinical evidence in favour of that diagnosis or differential diagnosis. It would also be important to recall if there were any contraindications. It is important to note that this explanation proceeds in the opposite direction to that taken when solving a clinical problem. Thus, when *arriving* at a decision, the doctor proceeds from clinical information to a diagnosis and then to a decision. However, when *explaining* a decision, it is more natural to describe the decision first, then the indication, and finally the clinical evidence.

The decision

The recipient of a request will not usually be told of the other options that have been considered and rejected. It is clear from the quantitative decision analysis described in Chapter 7 that, in order to explain the decision in detail, all the options that were considered must be described and also the reasons why one was chosen and the others rejected. However, when the doctor indicates the diagnosis that was the indication for the request, the recipient of the request will be able to guess from this diagnosis which other options would have been considered. In practice, most decisions are straightforward, many modern tests and treatments being reasonably safe. If there is a clear contraindication because of the patient's age or the presence of other conditions, there is often an acceptable alternative, so rules and guidelines can be applied to a reasonable proportion of decisions.

If there is doubt about the decision, the principles of quantitative decision analysis become useful when the decision is analysed, explained or checked in a non-quantitative way. In addition to specifying all the management options, the possible outcomes of each have to be considered, and their probability based on the various diagnoses which are present and the clinical evidence for them. Finally, the value (or utility) to the patient of each of these outcomes has to be taken into account, for which it is useful to have a summary of the patient's management, diagnoses and clinical evidence of the kind displayed in Table 1.

The diagnosis

A TIA would be a typical indication for prescribing aspirin. In this case, the indication is a diagnosis, but in other cases the indication may appear to be a finding. For example, if the procedure is a test, say, a request that the nurses make neurological observations, the indication might be 'recent facial weakness and hemiparesis'. However, this would be only a partial explanation because it does not specify the differential diagnoses which the test is attempting to resolve. These would be a TIA or a completed stroke, the former resolving within 24 hours, the latter persisting beyond that time. Thus, the 'grammar' of clinical explanations expects the doctor to specify the differential diagnoses (or at least one of them, e.g. 'possible TIA') when describing the indication for a test on a request form. The 'recent facial weakness and hemiparesis' should be regarded only as the evidence for the differential diagnoses.

Diagnoses are sometimes regarded as a convenient way of summarising the findings from a patient. Indeed, there may be a tendency sometimes to equate the diagnosis with a group of findings, for example, that TIA is regarded as a shorthand way of saying 'any transient neurological dysfunction that resolves within 24 hours'. However, a diagnosis is more than the sum of the evidence. It adds to the definitive or the sufficient diagnostic evidence by allowing the doctor to use his knowledge of the condition to infer or imagine the presence of other findings not yet discovered in that patient. These other findings may be discovered immediately if the appropriate action is taken (e.g. by performing a computerised tomography scan), they may be found only in future with or without treatment, or may not be observable directly (e.g. they may be inferred or imagined only as molecular changes in damaged neurons). If explanations are to be provided on computers, it is important to distinguish between a diagnosis and the clinical evidence for the diagnosis so that the software can be designed to handle information in a consistent way.

The presenting complaint

The first part of the clinical evidence to emphasise is the presenting complaint, for example, the sudden onset of a hemiparesis. In some cases, the presenting complaint may not be obvious, for example, the patient may have forgotten the original problem or be too ill or perhaps too embarrassed to describe it. An important factor to bear in mind is that the original symptoms will be used as important markers of progress and response to treatment, and it is therefore important to

Table 1. A 70-year-old patient presenting with transient neurological dysfunction.

Findings	Diagnosis	Management
Sudden weakness and clumsiness of left arm and face on day of admission, resolving within 24 hours. No history of migraine or fits. Blood sugar normal. CT scan: no mass.	**Transient ischaemic attack: right carotid distribution** ? due to atheromatous thromboembolism, originating from right internal carotid artery. ?? due to left atrial embolus.	Treatment of underlying cause (see below). Consider advising patient of increased risk of stroke and coronary events or withholding information.
Evidence of TIA. Bruit left side of neck.	**? Atheromatous thromboembolism from right internal carotid artery** ? due to carotid artery stenosis or atheromatous plaque. ? bilateral disease.	**Aspirin** 300 mg daily when BP controlled. ? For duplex ultrasound examination of carotids. If 70–90% stenosis, consider angiography and carotid endarterectomy. If 0–29%, not for surgery. If 30–69%, consider for European Carotid Surgery Trial.

BP	= blood pressure
CT	= computerised tomography
ECHO	= echoencephalography

clarify with the patient (or the next of kin) what he or she hopes to gain from the consultation. Although more objective measurements may become available later, which are more convenient and reliable from the doctor's point of view as markers of progress, it is clearly important not to lose sight of the original problem, and any formal decision process must take this into account. The presenting complaint may also have an important bearing on the scientific evidence available about a condition. For example, the data available on TIA will be based on a group of patients recruited to a study who had entry criteria of a particular type and severity. If the data on TIA were obtained from patients presenting in general practice with a wide spectrum of severity, the findings of that study may not apply to patients with more severe presentations who have been referred to hospital (see Chapter 5).

Table 1. *contd*

Findings	Diagnosis	Management
Pulse irregularly irregular. ECG: no P waves, irregular normal QRS complexes. ECHO: no valve abnormalities.	**Atrial fibrillation** ? causing cerebral embolus. Not due to valve disease. ? due to ischaemic heart disease.	**Aspirin** 300 mg daily when BP controlled. If not suitable for European Carotid Surgery Trial, consider for European Atrial Fibrillation Trial.
BP 200/120 mm Hg on admission. BP 170/105 mm Hg after one week. A-V nipping. Chest X-ray: big heart. ECG: left ventricular hypertrophy.	**Chronic hypertension** ? essential. ? due to renovascular disease.	Reduce calories, alcohol. Stop smoking. Atenolol 50 mg daily. Verapamil 80 mg three times per day.
Cholesterol 6.7 mmol/l.	**Mild hypercholesterol- aemia**	Reduce saturated fat intake.
VDRL negative.	No syphilis.	
ESR 20 mm/hour.	No arteritis.	

ESR   = erythrocyte sedimentation rate
TIA   = transient ischaemic attack
VDRL = Venereal Disease Research Laboratory test for syphilis

Diagnostic evidence

Definitive diagnostic evidence identifies all those—and only those—with a diagnosis. The 'gold standard test' is the test the result of which may yield the definitive evidence. 'Sufficient' diagnostic evidence identifies only those with a diagnosis, but not *all* those with the diagnosis. Some patients with the diagnosis will therefore have some other sufficient evidence. 'Diagnostic evidence' and 'diagnostic criterion' are broad terms used to describe both definitive and sufficient evidence. Occasionally, the presenting features are diagnostic (e.g. some 'spot' diagnoses in dermatology), but it is more usual to have to specify further items of information that form a definitive or sufficient combination of findings.

The term 'diagnostic' implies that the diagnosis is certain, which in turn implies the the probability of the expected outcome of implementing the decision based on the diagnosis is also high. Indeed, the definition of TIA depends on such an outcome: that is, that the neurological deficit resolves spontaneously within 24 hours. This is an important example. Most other diagnostic definitions are based on features present before the outcome becomes known, for example, microscopical appearances. 'Diagnostic' items of information may thus be regarded as no more than predictors of the outcome of the patient's illness with or without treatment, and the most important outcome markers are those original symptoms that can be explained by the diagnosis. In this sense, confirming a diagnosis is simply discovering the presence of some features regarded as diagnostic by convention because they are generally assumed to be consistent with one particular disease process and inconsistent with others. If many such conventional diagnostic combinations are available for a particular condition, any of these 'sufficient' combinations can be quoted to convince a colleague to accept a diagnosis without having to quote all the patient's findings.

The best diagnostic evidence

One of the most important functions of a diagnostic criterion is to identify those patients who are expected to benefit from the recognised treatment. In practice, a diagnostic criterion is usually assumed to be superior to other tests in this respect for theoretical reasons. Although it is possible to test this assumption, this is not done in a practical way at present. Thus, if the criterion is of no true value in identifying patients who will respond to treatment, for the patients 'identified' by the test result there would be no difference in outcome whether they were given placebo or active treatment. However, if the diagnostic criterion identifies only those who will respond, there would be a considerable difference in outcome between those given placebo and those given active treatment. Indeed, candidate diagnostic criteria could be ranked according to their performance as entry criteria for clinical trials of this kind. In many cases, gold standard tests provide numerical results, so there is also an issue of deciding the cut-off point separating those deemed to have the diagnosis from those who do not. In practice, the cut-off is assumed to be two standard deviations above the mean of a group of healthy subjects (perhaps of the same age and sex). A more appropriate approach, not part of clinical trial methodology at present, would be to vary the cut-off to see what effect this would have on the outcome of a placebo-controlled clinical trial.

Central evidence

If the diagnostic features of a TIA (i.e. complete resolution of an acute
neurological deficit within 24 hours) are not present, the evidence in
favour of the diagnosis will be a feature or combination of features
within which the frequency of patients with the diagnostic feature is
high (e.g. an acute hemiparesis with rapid improvement over six hours,
no past history of migraine, no fits, no fever, and normal blood sugar).
When 'frequency' knowledge of this kind about a group of patients is
applied to one particular patient it is converted into 'probability': the
probability of complete resolution of the acute neurological deficit in a
particular patient will thus be high. In practice, such observed frequencies are rarely documented formally. The probabilities used in clinical
practice are usually based on personal informal experience combined
with theoretical expectations. However, it is customary to quote the
minimum amount of clinical evidence required to demonstrate con-
vincingly that the probability of the diagnosis is high. If a small
combination of features (such as those given above) is known to be
highly predictive on its own, it may be used to summarise the probability,
given all the available evidence in the history, examination and test
results. This is known as the 'central evidence'[1] or the 'forceful feature'.[2]

Diagnosis by elimination

Highly predictive combinations of information are often assembled in
a logical way by applying a process referred to as 'diagnosis by
elimination'. For example, the causes of a sudden onset of a hemiparesis
would be a completed stroke, a TIA, complicated migraine, Todd's
paralysis, a cerebral abscess and hypoglycaemia. Rapid improvement
over six hours would exclude a completed stroke, absence of a past
history of migraine make complicated migraine less likely—and so on.
By pointing to evidence occurring frequently in those with a TIA but
less often in those with its differential diagnoses, the probability of a
TIA becomes correspondingly greater. Although this type of reasoning
has a logical flavour, it is not an application of logic in its narrow sense
of proceeding reliably from premises which are true (i.e. with a
probability of 1) to a true conclusion (also with a probability of 1).
Diagnosis by elimination is usually a special case of the probabilistic
reasoning described in Chapters 4 and 5. However, it is different to the
usual application of Bayes' theorem because it involves using only *one*
item of information to show that a particular differential diagnosis is
less likely. These individual items of information complement each
other so that when taken together they make the probability of a TIA
much higher. For this reasoning process to work reliably, the leads[3] (or

'pivots' as Eddy refers to them[4]) and eliminators[3] (or 'pruners' according to Eddy[4]) must have special characteristics in terms of likelihood ratios, prevalence of diseases and so on. The rules are therefore more complicated than they appear at first sight. If this type of reasoning is to be used reliably as a method of analysing, explaining, checking or justifying decisions objectively, it must be applied with care.[1,3]

Justifying decisions objectively

Some philosophers (the 'subjectivists') argue that objectivity is illusory, that all observations and decisions are based on some degree of subjectivity and that, as a result, objectivity is a matter of degree.[5] If objectivity is taken to mean the consistent application of a rule (chosen subjectively perhaps) in a planned way, the position becomes a little clearer. This definition would apply to observations and decisions made according to a planned protocol and to planned rules of logic or mathematics, respectively. Thus, if the rules for making or justifying a clinical decision are chosen before the observations are made, and not changed once the observations have begun, the decision will have been made 'objectively'. In practice, such an approach depends on intellectual integrity and a clear knowledge of the rules. The problem is twofold, in that the rules and guidelines may be difficult to remember and recall may be subconsciously selective. This latter problem affects medical audit because it is difficult to get doctors to take on board the lessons learnt from medical audit by changing their clinical practice; indeed, the same difficulty seems to apply to post-graduate medical education in general.

One way to check clinical decisions objectively would be to build the rules or guidelines into a computer system which is used to request tests and treatments. Each time a doctor wishes to implement a decision by making such a request, he or she would enter the clinical details into a window on the screen by choosing the various entries from a series of 'pick-lists' which appear automatically. The items to be entered would be the diagnostic indications (and contraindications) and the clinical evidence for each diagnosis. This would allow the doctor to check all decisions before implementing them. He or she would also be collecting information which could be used to display a summary of the patient's progress at any time (see Table 1), for example, immediately on discharge from hospital or when the patient leaves the outpatient clinic or general practitioner's surgery.

It must be emphasised that this approach addresses the question of analysing, explaining, justifying and checking decisions *that have already been made subjectively* and does not interfere with the original decision making process. Furthermore, it can be applied only to situations sufficiently well recognised and straightforward to be represented by rules or guidelines. If a decision cannot be explained or justified in this way, then an inability to explain using guidelines merely draws attention to the decision so that it can be reviewed. For example, the decision to prescribe aspirin could be explained by pointing to the occurrence of a TIA but, on the other hand, it would also be contraindicated by the presence of hypertension and the patient's age. A simple rule of justification would depend on the presence of a clear indication and the absence of any contraindication to aspirin. Decision analysis as explained in Chapter 7 is designed to be used in situations of this kind that cannot be covered by a set of pre-arranged rules or guidelines.

The way in which the decision analysis was carried out in Chapter 7 was highly subjective. The utilities were chosen to reflect the patient's feelings or those of the doctor who was trying to represent her. In this context, therefore, the decision analysis was performed as a subjective second opinion by breaking down the problem into a number of components and attaching subjective probabilities to the diagnoses and outcomes, and also by allocating utilities to the latter. Once these values had been added, the calculations were carried out in a planned and objective way. If it were possible to allocate the probabilities and utilities objectively (by basing them on careful population studies conducted in a planned way with clear rules), the decision analysis would also be objective.

The appeal of an objective decision is that it is thought to be free of human fallibility and in this way might guarantee some minimum level of performance. On the other hand, a decision independent of human control may be equally threatening. A subjective human decision combined with an objective decision would seem to give the best of both worlds. Thus, if independent reasoning methods lead to the same conclusion, in general there would be an increased expectation of a successful outcome.

The expert's system

Before a decision can be analysed, explained or checked, it must have been made by someone with a degree of expertise. A computer system used in this way can thus be called an 'expert's system' (note the apostrophe). In contrast, the term 'medical expert system' (note there is no apostrophe) implies that the medical expert's performance is being imitated by the computer programme. This is achieved by analysing what the medical expert does and incorporating his knowledge and reasoning processes into a computer programme.[6] In contrast, the expert's system would provide expertise in analysing, explaining and checking a decision, as opposed to solving the medical problem. It could also be used to provide expertise in running clinical studies, and recording and managing data—a service of considerable benefit to a busy doctor who would like to be able to do these things, but who may be distracted by the demands of clinical care. Audit could be made more sophisticated by prompting the doctor to specify the probability of the outcome of each decision, and then to compare the expected outcome with what actually happened.

Keeping a record of expectations and outcomes

A record of clinical decisions and their outcomes could be kept by designing computerised request forms with space for the physician to indicate the expected outcome of the test and also the probability with which this outcome was expected. This would give the recipient of the form a clearer indication of the sender's expectations. This could also be done on prescriptions but, instead of specifying a test result, the prescriber would specify the expected outcome. For example, if a hypotensive agent was being given, the target blood pressure could be specified (e.g. less than 145/90 mm Hg), together with the probability of achieving this. A number of other target outcomes could also be specified (e.g. no side-effects to the drug), the probability of which could also be specified. The actual result of the test or response to treatment could then be compared with the expected result.

The expected and real outcomes could be analysed in a number of ways. The simplest analysis would be to compare the overall and expected frequencies of outcome. The latter could be based on the average of all the individual probabilities of the expected outcomes. Another way of analysing the results would be to construct a calibration curve, from which the frequency with which the predicted outcome occurred for any specified probability could be read. Thus, in the sub-group of patients in whom the target blood pressure was expected to be achieved with a probability of 90%, in the long run 90% of them should actually achieve this target.[2] It might be tiresome to do all this for every clinical situation, and the approach might be acceptable to many doctors only if it was done as part of a clinical audit carried out for a limited length of time.

Reminders about clinical management and research

A prescribing doctor who is faced with an awkward situation, might be offered automatically the services of an expert system or be invited to read about the problem on a page of text held on the computer which discussed prescribing aspirin for patients with TIAs, for example. He might also be invited to use an expert system which would take him through a clinical decision analysis of the expected costs and benefits of carotid angiography and carotid endarterectomy in an older hypertensive patient with atrial fibrillation. Although medical expert systems are often thought of in popular terms as computerised medical consultants, the techniques used in them can be used to present all kinds of information in a way which is more convenient to the user of computers.[6] They could, for example, guide the user through a decision analysis of a difficult clinical problem which may involve calculating diagnostic probabilities. In this way, many techniques which appear to rival each other at present may in due course come to complement each other.

A message might appear on the screen reminding the prescribing doctor that the patient was eligible for a drug trial, for example, the European Atrial Fibrillation or European Carotid Artery trials. The doctor might then ask for a printout of the pre-entry forms for the trial to see whether the patient satisfied the criteria for entry. The information could be entered automatically into the computer terminal, and at any time the doctor could decide to print out a summary of the patient's findings, diagnoses and management (which would have been created automatically from information entered already).

Medical audit

By explaining, justifying, and therefore checking discussions on a computer system as he went along, the physician would be conducting a 'concurrent audit', and also providing ample data for retrospective audit. It would be possible to find out what proportion of decisions were made in accordance with planned guidelines, and to highlight for discussion later those which went against guidelines. If more details were required, for example, an audit of stroke patients' perception of their own progress, the appropriate form could be printed out automatically as soon as the diagnosis was entered into the computer.

Conclusion

Modern medicine is complicated, and many things can go wrong. There is a danger that decision analysis, formal decision methods, expert systems and computers in general might make the doctor's life even more complicated than it is at present. However, if these techniques can be used to simplify and speed up form filling, to explain, justify and check decisions as we go along, produce medical summaries automatically, and help organise research, medical audit and resource management, they may well become a cost-effective proposition.

References

1. Llewelyn DEH. *Assessing the validity of diagnostic tests and clinical decisions.* MD thesis, University of London, 1987
2. Gale J, Marsden P. *Medical diagnosis, from students to physician.* Oxford: Oxford University Press, 1983
3. Llewelyn DEH. Mathematical analysis of the diagnostic relevance of clinical findings. *Clinical Science* 1979; **57**: 477–9
4. Eddy DM, Clanton CH. The art of diagnosis: solving the clinicopathological conference. *New England Journal of Medicine* 1982; **306**: 1263–8
5. Lacey AR. *A dictionary of philosophy.* London: Routledge and Kegan Paul, 1980
6. Fox J. Formal and knowledge based methods in decision technology. *Acta Psychologica* 1984; **56**: 303–31 (also in: Dowie J, Elstein A, eds. *Professional judgement, a reader in clinical decision making.* Cambridge: Cambridge University Press, 1988)

APPENDIX 1

Clinical decision analysis: an application to the management of an elderly person with hypertension who has had a transient ischaemic attack (see Chapter 7)

This appendix contains all the sections of the decision tree analysed in Chapter 7, but for which only the branch for 'antihypertensives only' was presented.

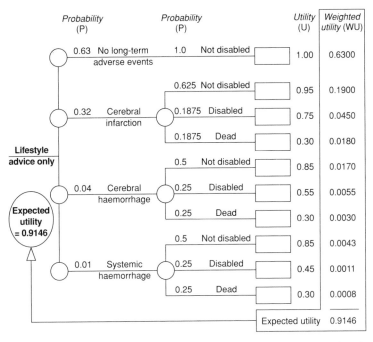

Fig. A. *The branch of the decision tree which shows how the expected utility was calculated for lifestyle advice only.*

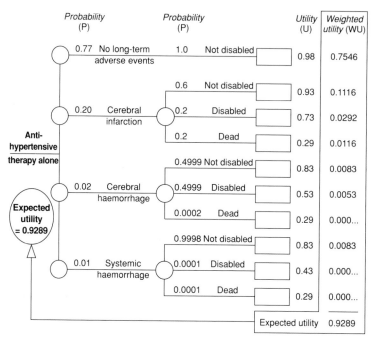

Fig. B. *The branch of the decision tree which shows how the expected utility was calculated for antihypertensive therapy only.*

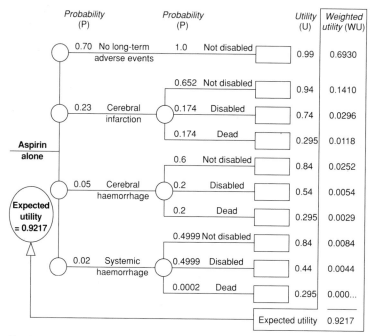

Fig. C. *The branch of the decision tree which shows how the expected utility was calculated for aspirin alone.*

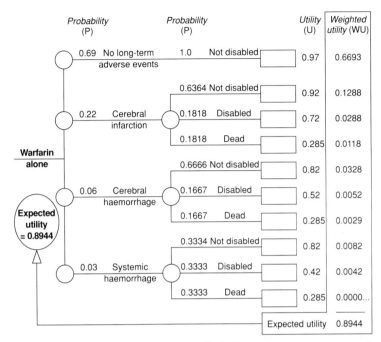

Fig. D. *The branch of the decision tree which shows how the expected utility was calculated for warfarin alone.*

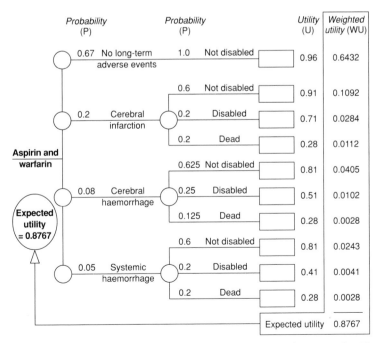

Fig. E. *The branch of the decision tree which shows how the expected utility was calculated for aspirin and warfarin.*

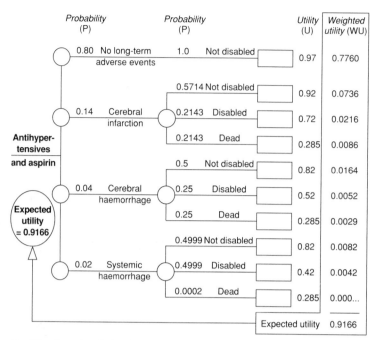

Fig. F. *The branch of the decision tree which shows how the expected utility was calculated for antihypertensive therapy and aspirin.*

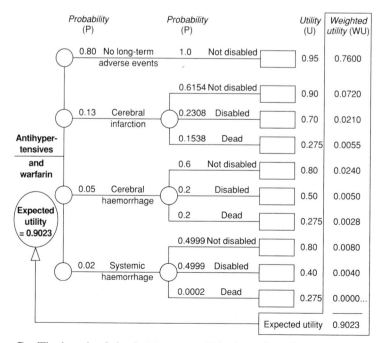

Fig. G. *The branch of the decision tree which shows how the expected utility was calculated for antihypertensive therapy and warfarin.*

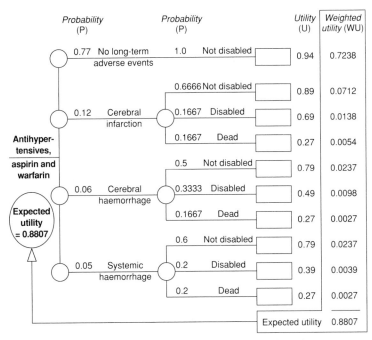

Fig. H. *The branch of the decision tree which shows how the expected utility was calculated for antihypertensive therapy, aspirin and warfarin.*

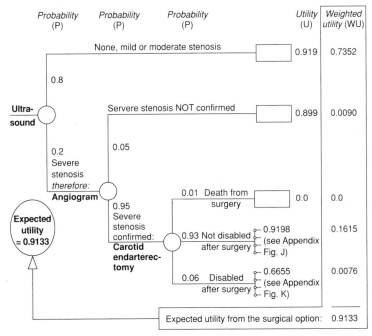

Fig. I. *The branch of the decision tree which shows how the expected utility was calculated for surgical management.*

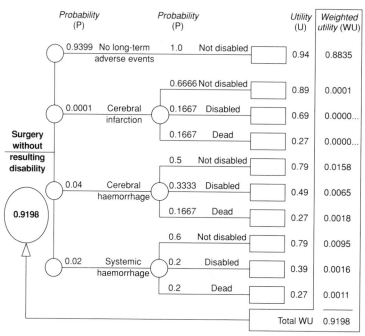

Fig. J. *The sub-tree for surgery without resulting disability.*

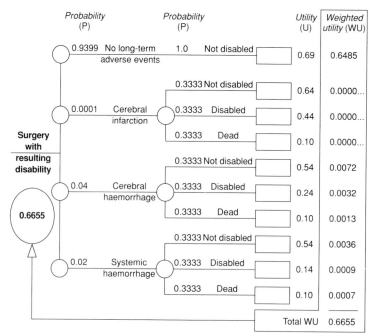

Fig. K. *The sub-tree for surgery with resulting disability.*

APPENDIX 2
Members of the Workshop
(in alphabetical order)

Dr Sterling Bryan Health Economics Research Group, The University of West London

Dr Lucio Capurso Department of Gastroenterology, General Hospital, S. Filippo Neri, Rome, Italy

Professor AP Dawid Department of Statistical Science, University College, London

Professor F Tim de Dombal Director, Clinical Information Science Unit, University of Leeds

Professor David M Denison National Heart and Lung Institute, London

Dr Jack Dowie Senior Lecturer, Faculty of Social Sciences, The Open University, Milton Keynes

Professor Michael Drummond Professor of Economics, Centre for Health Economics, University of York

Dr David AW Edwards 18 Copthall Gardens, Mill Hill, London

Dr Peter A Emerson Honorary Consultant Physician, Chelsea and Westminster Hospital; Director, Riverside Unit, Coding and Clinical Information System Development Project, London

Dr C Fenn G D Searle Limited, High Wycombe, Bucks

Mr Richard Godfrey National Heart and Lung Institute, London

Dr Graeme Hankey Department of Clinical Neurosciences, Western General Hospital, Edinburgh

Dr Anthony Hopkins Director, Research Unit, Royal College of Physicians, London

Dr Beverley Hunt Department of Haematology, St Thomas's Hospital, London

Dr Robin P Knill-Jones Senior Lecturer in Epidemiology, Department of Public Health, University of Glasgow

Professor Maurizio Koch Department of Gastroenterology, General Hospital, S. Filippo Neri, Rome, Italy

Dr Huw Llewelyn Senior Lecturer, Department of Medicine, School of Medicine and Dentistry of King's College, London

Dr Elizabeth J Maher Regional Centre for Radiotherapy and Oncology, Mount Vernon Hospital, Northwood, Middlesex

Dr Charles FA Pantin Respiratory Physiology Department, City General Hospital, Stoke-on-Trent

Dr Martin P Severs Department of Geriatrics, St Mary's Hospital, Portsmouth

Mr James M Slattery Medical Statistician, Neurosciences Trials Unit, Department of Clinical Neurosciences, Western General Hospital, Edinburgh

Professor Charles P Warlow Professor of Neurology, University Department of Clinical Neurosciences, Northern General Hospital, Edinburgh

Dr John G Williams School of Postgraduate Studies in Medical and Health Care, University College of Swansea